Helping Your Child Handle STRESS

The Parent's Guide to Recognizing and Solving Childhood Problems

- *Fussy Eater*
- *Constipation*
- *Chaotic Mealtimes*
- *Weight Problems*
- *New Baby*
- *School Problems*
- *Parental Expectations*
- *Homework*
- *Learning Problems*
- *Starting School*
- *Leaving Home*
- *Moodiness*
- *Suicidal Tendencies*
- *A Child's Illness*
- *A Parent's Illness*
- *Handicaps*
- *Temptations*
- *Responsibilities*
- *Custody Problems*
- *Single Parent*
- *Kidnapping*

Helping Your Child Handle STRESS

The Parent's Guide to Recognizing and Solving Childhood Problems

Katharine Kersey, Ed.D.
Author of *Sensitive Parenting*

ACROPOLIS BOOKS LTD.
WASHINGTON, D.C.

Dedicated to

my friend, Fae

April 11, 1930–October 6, 1985

who shared my life with me and

who would loved to have

seen this book in print

ACROPOLIS BOOKS, LTD.
Colortone Building, 2400 17th St., N.W.,
Washington, D.C. 20009

Printed in the United States of America by
COLORTONE PRESS
Creative Graphics, Inc.
Washington, D.C. 20009

Attention: Schools and Corporations
ACROPOLIS books are available at quantity discounts with bulk purchase for educational, business, or sales promotional use. For information, please write to: SPECIAL SALES DEPARTMENT, ACROPOLIS BOOKS LTD., 2400 17th ST., N.W., WASHINGTON, D.C. 20009

Are there Acropolis Books you want but cannot find in your local stores?
You can get any Acropolis book title in print. Simply send title and retail price, plus $1.50 cents per copy to cover mailing and handling costs for each book desired. District of Columbia residents add applicable sales tax. Enclose check or money order only, no cash please, to: ACROPOLIS BOOKS LTD., 2400 17th ST., N.W., WASHINGTON, D.C. 20009.

Special thanks to the many families who shared their photographs for inclusion in this book.

Library of Congress Cataloging-in-Publication Data

Kersey, Katharine C., 1935–
   Helping your child handle stress.

   1. Stress in children. 2. Child rearing. I. Title.
BF723.S75K47   1985   155.4   85-22842
ISBN 0-87491-791-3

Acknowledgments

I am especially grateful to two former teaching assistants who have meant a lot to me personally, who have encouraged and challenged me and who have joined me in my efforts to make the world a better place for children.

To Amy Reese, I say a special thank-you for spending long hours in many libraries collecting and reading books to be used in the selected bibliographies at the end of each chapter.

To Susan Vorhis, another very big thank-you for opening her heart and home to me and spending many tireless days and nights helping me pull together thoughts and ideas to shape them into the chapters found in this book.

I wish to express gratitude to my own parents who instilled in me the desire to pursue meaningful work and to my husband who is patient and accepting of my needs.

I also want to thank the hundreds of other people, including my students, who have had faith in me and shared their life stories—who have opened my eyes to this fascinating and challenging field and given me the desire to look for answers to some of these life problems which affect all of us at one time or another.

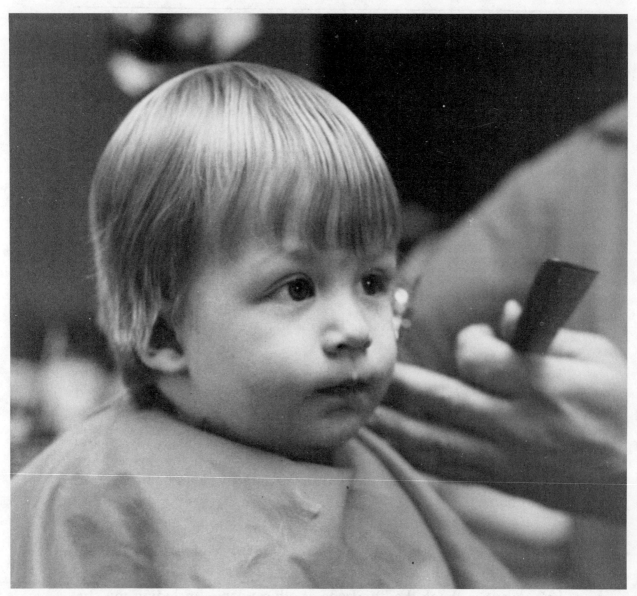

Letting a child know ahead of time what to expect helps him to accept and adjust to new experiences.

Preface

*H*elping *Your Child Handle Stress* is a guide for parents on heading off unnecessary problems and coping with those that are unavoidable.

No parent should try to raise children in a stress-free world or to shield them from the realities of life. Instead, your goal should be to give your children inner skills and strengths, so they can handle the challenges ahead. We know that our children will trip and fall at times, but we want to teach them how to pick themselves up, how to turn problems into opportunities, and stumbling blocks into stepping stones.

This book is not meant to be a complete discussion of each of the problems our children are likely to encounter. It is an introduction to these problems for parents who want to prevent normal and abnormal stresses from becoming lifelong afflictions. It is meant to help you recognize the symptoms of a serious crisis before permanent damage is done.

When a baby enters the family, there will always
be a certain amount of stress. This new event
requires adjustment, change, and reorientation.

Contents

Bringing up children in a healthy environment is a balancing act. We want to give our children a stimulating environment, a good education, and situations and challenges that will help them grow.

Introduction

The Parent's Role in Helping Children Handle Stress

When a baby enters the family, there will always be a certain amount of stress. This new event requires adjustment, change, and reorientation.

As the child grows, his simultaneous need for protection and independence may confuse the average parent.

Usually, the child indicates his readiness for new challenges by demonstrating interest in and a growing ability to handle new situations. Sometimes, the parent is ready before the child. Other times, the child is ready before the parent. If not handled wisely, these confusing times can be quite stressful.

When a young child is unduly stressed, he usually regresses. He reverts to babyish behavior—whining, crying, clinging, and demanding.

Often, when he is expending a great deal of energy trying to master a new skill, he becomes disagreeable, unpredictable, and unpleasant. As soon as he accomplishes his goal, his normal disposition usually returns.

If a child appears to be stuck in his regressed state and shows no signs of recovery, it is probably time to take a look at the way the situation is being handled.

Since a child does not have a clear view of himself as a person or see how he fits into the world, he is very much dependent on the adults around him to give him his sense of self and show him the way to maturity.

Children are even more vulnerable to stress than is an adult, because they do not have past histories to help them put life in perspective. Serious events and traumas can affect them in negative ways or make them stronger individuals better equipped to handle future upsets and challenges.

Bringing up children in a healthy environment is a balancing act. We want to give our children a stimulating environment, a good education, and situations and challenges that will be tough enough to stimulate them to find alternatives to solving life's problems. Each of these new demands creates some stress. If the child can master the problem, the stress lessens. The next time the child is faced with a similar problem, he knows how to handle it better. He gradually learns to generalize his solutions to other problems, thus increasing his coping skills and feelings of control.

If one can figure out constructive ways to handle the stress, the stress reaction is manageable. Chronic, continuing doubt, fear, or uncertainty, however, can lead to serious consequences for mental as well as physical health. Diseases associated with stress include high blood pressure, peptic ulcers, kidney diseases, colitis, asthma, diabetes, headaches, rheumatic fever, rheumatoid arthritis, and perhaps cancer.

If the child is confronted with too many stressful situations or if these stresses are too severe, the strain will become too great to handle, and the experience will take its toll.

Children often cannot tell us what they are feeling. Instead, they show us through their behavior how they are feeling about their stresses and hurts.

Below are some of the trouble signs seen in children to overly stressful situations. It is important to remember that each child is different and that many of the coping mechanisms he chooses are those he sees in the behavior of the significant adults who care for him.

Birth to age three

Regression (toilet training, whining, tearfulness, babyish ways)

Increased separation anxieties

Sleep problems

Excessive masturbation

Increased tantrums

Aggression

Increased possessiveness
    (of toys, belongings, and people)

Withdrawal or apathy

Preschool

Irritability, whining, tearfulness

"Too good" behavior

Aggression

Increased fantasy (things are as they used to be or as they want them to be)

Increased need for physical contact

Despondency, sadness, longing for the past

Self-blame and self-accusation

Phobias and compulsions

At preschool: restlessness, distractibility, fears of failure, excessive daydreaming, poor peer relations

Middle years (six-twelve)

Open suffering (sadness and grieving)

Worry and fear about present and future

Feeling responsible for past, present, and future

Great conflict (guilt)

Anger (expressed and unexpressed)

Seeming bravado and courage

Taking matters into own hands (trying to solve adult problems)

Adolescence

Open hostility

Acting-out behavior

Defiance—lashing out in talk and behavior

Need for blame

Shame

Sensitivity

Mood swings

School difficulties (drop in achievement)

Aggression or withdrawal

Difficulty with peers

Shift of dependency onto others (friends or person of the
opposite sex)

Eating problems (anorexia, bulimia, overeating)

Parents and other interested adults can help children learn to cope with stress. The strategies below apply to children of all ages and can be used effectively for many different situations as long as the child's age, personality, and maturity are taken into consideration.

- Understand the child's level of development. Look for symptoms of stress. Don't punish the child for symptomatic behavior.

- Expect regression, changes, problems, and anger.

- *Listen.* Clear up misconceptions. Listen for clues in his talk with others, play, etc. Encourage verbal expressions of anger.

- *Talk* with the child—a lot. Don't assume that because he hasn't mentioned it, it isn't on his mind. You may need to encourage him to talk.

- Tell him the truth. Tell him how you feel. He will know how to cope better if he understands that you are having difficulty, too. Remember that the way your child handles a challenge will largely be determined by the way you handle it.

- Reassure the child. Tell him what he can expect in the future.

- Encourage him to express opinions, suggestions, and solutions for the future.

- Reassure him of the normalcy of his feelings. Expose him to other children his age with the same problems.

- Provide substitute relationships for him. Let others help out (grandparents, Big Brothers/Big Sisters, relatives, friends, neighbors, church groups). Seek professional help, if necessary.

- Encourage his development of competence and independence.

- Keep in touch with his school. Talk with his teacher.

- Reassure the child of parental love, support, and constancy.

- Meet your own needs. Don't depend on the child to do it for you. Get help if you need it.

A meaningful relationship with an adult is the single most important factor in determining the future mental health of any child. Every child needs to have at least one adult who thinks he is wonderful, who really cares what happens to him, and who gives freely of his time and energy to the child while he is young. The mental health of the significant adult will be modeled by the child, and the child will grow up to internalize the coping skills he learned through observation and imitation.

There are many excellent books written for adults and children facing various stresses in their lives. I have listed some of them at the end of each chapter. Take the time to go to the library or bookstore with the child to select books which are appropriate for his level of development and understanding. Then, read the books together. They can often open up roads to communication that might never have been revealed otherwise.

The problems described in this book were chosen because of their seriousness and potentially serious consequences they can have on a child's life if ignored. More importantly, however, is to show the positive influences stress can have in a child's life if the adults in charge understand the child, his level of understanding and development, and learn techniques to make the child stronger, more compassionate, and capable.

Children learn through discovery and need adults to provide new opportunities and experiences.

Chapter One

Toilet Training

The topic of toilet training often panics an otherwise self-assured and calm parent. If toilet training is smooth and uneventful it can bring a sense of accomplishment and satisfaction to all concerned, but if it is mishandled, it can become a disastrous battleground.

Generally, if you wait until the child is ready (roughly two years of age), and if you do not become emotionally involved in his successes or failures, toilet training will be accomplished with a limited amount of frustration and hassle.

Resistance

However, if you start too early or put too much pressure on the child, he may:

- feel helpless, inadequate, or frustrated;
- develop fears, shyness, or nightmares;
- become generally balky, resistant, and rebellious;
- develop eating problems;
- learn that he can control you; or

- develop constipation and/or bed–wetting problems that can last for years.

You can tell that a child is ready to begin toilet training when he:

- can talk fairly well;
- stays dry for several hours at a time; and
- shows signs that he is able to *anticipate* bathroom needs— wiggling, holding himself, or becoming restless.

Bowel training usually comes before bladder training. Some suggestions for success:

- Teach the child words to use to identify his bathroom products. (It is best not to use words like "dirty" which give him a negative opinion about his natural functions.)
- Use these words when you know he is having a bowel movement and again when you change his diapers.
- Put a potty chair in the bathroom and let him play with it and try it out before you show him what it is for. (Children sometimes are frightened by the height of a toilet seat or the force of a flushing toilet.)
- If it doesn't bother you, it is helpful if he observes others (especially older children) using the bathroom.
- Watch for the child's own biological signals. Do not try to decide when the child needs to have a bowel movement (e.g., every day after breakfast). If we teach him to ignore his internal signals, he may lose them altogether and have difficulty all his life in recognizing his automatic call to the bathroom.
- Dress him in training pants. Let him learn to pull them down and up himself. Leave a clean supply where he can reach them. Take him to the bathroom when he "looks" ready.
- Reinforce first successes with praise and affection. *Ignore failures. Do not punish accidents*. Be prepared for clean-ups.

- Wait until the child has left the bathroom to flush the contents of the toilet. Sometimes, children are frightened by noisy machines that make things disappear.

- Let him use the adult's toilet and those away from home so he won't become dependent upon familiar conditions.

- Do all you can to convince him that he will be able to master toilet training. Help him to realize that it is up to him, not you. When he does succeed, he will be proud of himself.

Bladder control is generally harder for the child to establish than bowel control, because it is easier for a child to make something happen than to stop something from happening. There are two aspects of bladder control: waking and sleeping control. Waking control usually comes first.

There are three stages which must be accomplished, in order, before a child is ready for bladder control:

> Stage 1—He knows that he has urinated.
>
> Stage 2—He knows that he is urinating.
>
> Stage 3—He knows that he needs to urinate.

When the child has arrived at the third stage, the parent can safely begin to teach bladder control.

- Put the child in training pants. Tell him that he can urinate in the toilet.

- Depend on his own biological signal that he needs to urinate. Wait until his bladder is full. Don't try him too often. He needs to learn and listen to his internal signals.

- Boys seem to learn best by standing up. If girls want to try this way, let them. They will discover quickly that it doesn't work as well for them.

- Use sensible words for biological functions, not confusing euphemisms like "Go see Mrs. Jones."

- Encourage independence. Let him go by himself. Don't teach him to tell you when he has to go.

- Reward successes with praise, hugs, or a small treat. Something tangible often makes a greater impression and gets the process underway more quickly. As soon as the habit is well established, the reward can be gradually diminished or withdrawn, until it is no longer needed.

- Expect slip-ups. Ignore failures and accidents.

- If, after a week or ten days, attempts at bladder control don't seem to be working, give up and go back to diapers. Wait a few months before you try again.

Regression

Eleann had to go to traffic court and, having no one to keep three-year-old Kathy and one-year-old Dawn, she took them with her. While she was waiting to be called, Kathy, who was still wearing diapers, started to tell her mother that she had to go to the bathroom. Eleann said that she could not leave the courtroom. Kathy started crying, first softly, then louder, that she had to use the toilet.

Embarrassed that others would hear her daughter's demands, Eleann finally decided to risk missing her name being called and left the courtroom with the two girls. She began the search for a bathroom. When they finally located it, and Eleann removed Kathy's diapers, she found them already wet. Kathy said that she could't wait and now she didn't have to "go" anymore.

Eleann was angry and confused. She had been very inconvenienced by Kathy's demands and already worn out from trying to "do the right thing." Once again, Kathy had gotten the best of her on the toilet-training routine. Frustrated, she spanked Kathy and hurried them all back into the courtroom, hoping that her name had not been called. Kathy was now more upset and crying loudly, embarrassing her mother even more.

It is unfortunate that Eleann had to take the children with her to traffic court. Kathy was probably testing her mother to see if she could get some additional attention. She could also have been bored and decided that a trip to the bathroom would be an interesting diversion. Since Eleann knew that Kathy was in diapers, she could have told her that they could not leave now and that it would be all right for her to urinate in her diapers. She might also have provided some reserve surprises, kept in her pocket book for emergencies, and promised her a treat if she could remain quiet and obedient until they could leave.

These kinds of situations are different for parents and, ideally, should be well thought out ahead of time. The child needs to be prepared for a long, boring wait, and parents must be well equipped for the ordeal with raisins, orange juice, toys, books, crayons, and scratch paper.

Oftentimes, toilet training becomes a battleground with young children. It is up to the parents to make sure that the child does not get attention and reinforcement for uncooperative behavior.

Eleann should have withdrawn from the battle completely. She could tell Kathy that, from now on, whether or not she uses the toilet is completely up to her. If she chooses to use the toilet, she may wear training pants, and if she chooses not to, she may wear diapers. She should continue to use diapers without any lectures, fussing, or discussion about it. If Kathy insists on training pants, Eleann could tell her that they will try them in a few days. The child should want to make the transition herself. If she has an accident, the training pants should be removed without fuss or disapproval and the diapers put back on. The less she hears about the subject, the better. I would not even discuss this matter in front of her with father, grandparents, siblings, or friends.

It sometimes helps to put diapers back on completely and tell the child that on her next birthday she may start wearing training pants. Take her to the store to help select the pants and then choose the drawer in which to keep them. She can show them off to her friends and relatives and brag about the fact that on her birthday she is going to start wearing them. This often works very successfully. It convinces the child ahead of time that she will be able to control her functions and it gives her an incentive for doing so.

Many parents are uncertain about trying to toilet train their children. They hear conflicting messages from well-meaning grandparents, friends, and neighbors about the best age to start and the most successful method to use. Sometimes they allow the *process* to become too important and get caught up in power struggles that then, unintentionally, teach the child that he can control them with his performance or refusal to perform. They intermittently reinforce accidents and failure by becoming excited, upset or punitive, thus inadvertently creating problems that can last for years.

Children get very confused when adults give so much attention to toilet training, when it gets to be the most talked about subject of the day, and when they receive inconsistent attention for their accidents. If parents will "let up" and allow the child the dignity to regress if he needs to, they will find that he will soon come around and decide that it is more rewarding to behave in age appropriate ways.

Bed-wetting

Since Ross, 6, had been a bed-wetter ever since he was out of diapers, the family had developed a regular nighttime procedure. Ross was allowed only one glass of liquid for supper and none after 7 p.m. Every night, he asked for something to drink, and, every night, his parents told him that he couldn't have anything because he still wet the bed. When it was time to go to bed, they reminded him to use the toilet. Then, when they went to bed, they got him up and took him one last time— usually sleepy and grumpy and sometimes most uncooperative.

This night was no exception. All the routine had proceeded as usual, and, at 3 a.m., Ross appeared at his parents' bed, announcing that he was wet and needed his bed changed. His mother told him to sleep on the other side of the bed, but Ross complained loudly that it was wet, too, and pulled on her covers, begging her to get up.

Finally she struggled out of bed and performed the nightly ritual, fussing and complaining to Ross that she couldn't understand why he did this to her. She got out some clean pajamas for him and changed his sheets. She felt confused and guilty. She wasn't sure whether he could help it or not, so her reactions were inconsistent. Sometimes she was accepting, and, at other times, she couldn't help being irritable and angry.

Bed-wetting (enuresis) has many causes and no easy solutions. Since one of its causes can be faulty toilet training, it makes sense to follow a relaxed and gradual progression from waking control to sleeping control.

After the child has established good daytime control, then he can be put in training pants at night. Expect some wet clothes and sheets. Be patient. When the bed is wet, change the bedding casually, saying, "Next time, maybe you can wake up and use the toilet." When children have been trained by the relaxed method prescribed earlier, nighttime control usually follows in a reasonable amount of time.

However, there are many factors that can delay nighttime control:

- bladder disfunction or disease;
- too much pressure put on the child for daytime control or for growing up too soon in other ways;
- illness, stress, a new baby, the loss of a parent or loved one, a move to a new location or new school;
- divorce or perceived loss of support from a significant adult;
- physical abuse;
- sexual stimulation and confusion or ambivalence over sex identity;
- need to retaliate and inability to show anger in any other way.

When a child who has stayed dry for several years suddenly begins wetting the bed, there is usually a reason. Look for some kind of new stress: a move, or starting a new school, for example. I feel strongly that, when parents sense a change in the behavior or disposition of their child, it is up to them to look for a cause and take steps to correct the situation. They may choose to help the child cope with the new stress or to change the environment altogether. If children are forced to "stick out" a situation that is hopeless, demeaning, or debilitating to them, parents often regret it. When they look back, they see that those problems caused more severe ones later.

Bed-wetting can become a habit if a child receives a lot of attention because of it. In these cases bed-wetting is the one trait that makes him different from his sibling(s). A wise parent will work hard to help the child find a more productive area of distinction—such as learning to play an instrument or ski or become an expert on birds. Often when a child develops an expertise that earns him the attention he craves, he will abandon the less desirable behavior.

Remember:

- A child does not consciously wet his bed. (He is, after all, asleep!)

- Bed-wetting often runs in families. The parent who had the same problem himself may be less able to deal with it effectively in his child, because it reminds him of his own childhood; or more able to accept it because it seems normal.

- Children do not wet their beds because they sleep more soundly. Experts have found that non-bed-wetters are no easier to arouse than bed-wetters, and there is no difference in the electroencephalographic patterns of the two groups.

- Decreasing fluid intake will not solve the problem.

- Bed-wetting may be serving a special purpose for the child that he is not ready to give up.

- Punishment does not help.

- Bed-wetters come to feel that there is something wrong with them. They usually conclude that they are somehow different, deficient, or damaged.

The problem often perpetuates itself and can affect the child's self concept and his ability to learn. If bed-wetting is ignored, the child may conclude that he is the only one who wets his bed and that his parents feel sorry for him and believe that he cannot be cured. For this reason, bed–wetting is a problem that should be addressed.

Gary, 9, had gone to spend the night at the home of his friend, Bruce. Jane had been in bed for hours when the phone rang. It took a little while for her to identify the voice at the other end. She had forgotten temporarily that Gary was not at home, so she didn't recognize his voice when she heard him crying, "Mom, will you come and get me?"

"What's wrong, Gary?" she asked when she was awake enough to figure out what was going on.

"I wet the bed and I want to come home."

"Does anyone know you are calling me?" she asked.

"No, they are all asleep. Hurry up, please," he begged.

Jane was in a dilemma. She knew that if she went to get Gary, he would have to tell his friend's mother that he was leaving. Still, she felt sorry for him. She wished that she had never let him go, knowing that he still wet the bed frequently. She had hoped that it would not happen away from home.

"I'll bring you some clean pajamas, Gary. I think you had better stay at Bruce's though, because they will be worried to death in the morning to find you gone."

She hung up and drove to Bruce's home, taking a change of clothes for Gary. He was waiting for her on the front steps.

Spending the night with friends can be a disastrous experience for a child who still wets his bed. Let him carry his own sleeping bag, a change of pajamas, and a plastic bag for his wet clothes whenever he goes visiting. Warn the friend's mother about the bed-wetting problem, so your child won't be embarrassed by having to talk about it.

Here are a few more suggestions:

- Check with your pediatrician to make certain that there are no physical problems that could be corrected. Most doctors will not recommend extensive hospital testing because of their long-term experience with such procedures and their fear of intensifying the importance of the problem for the child. However, I would certainly take your doctor's advice in the matter.

- Talk with your child about his bed-wetting. Try to make it clear to him that:
  —there is nothing wrong with him;
  —there are many others with the same problem;
  —he will outgrow it;
  —it does not alter the way you feel about him;
  —it is safe for him to express feelings (bad as well as good).
  —you are willing to help him.

- Try offering an incentive for breaking the bed-wetting habit. Let him negotiate the agreement. Make a chart: for every dry night, he receives a point. For each five points, he will receive a new stamp for his stamp collection. When he has accumulated fifty points, he will receive something he has wanted for a long time (basketball goal, guitar, or a puppy). It could be that it has merely become a habit now, and habits are hard to break. Offering him a reward—something that he wants badly—might be enough to make it worth the effort needed to wake himself up. If he is not interested in such a program now, remind him that he may be interested later. If so, he can let you know.

Chronic Constipation

Donna and Clay had been having problems in their marriage for several years. There had been many fights, both physical and verbal, and many unpleasant episodes.

Finally they had agreed to split, and Clay had moved out. The battles did not stop, though, and four-year-old Jerry witnessed awful scenes in person and heard many more over the telephone.

Although Jerry had been completely toilet trained before he was three, recently he had begun having accidents.

That was the last thing Donna needed, so she decided to put a stop to it. She spanked Jerry hard whenever he moved his bowels in his pants and threatened to make him wear diapers to school.

Jerry stopped having bowel movements during the daytime. About once a week, he had diarrhea in his bed while he slept.

Donna called the doctor and punished her son. Nothing seemed to help.

Children can develop severe constipation or soiling problems (encopresis) when there is added stress in their lives. There are many reasons why this can happen (such as reaction to punishment, power struggles, hostility, fear, or unsuccessful toilet training), but a child who shows such symptoms should be seen by a physician.

Sometimes, if the pressure is taken off of the child (and no fuss is made when his accidents occur), the problem goes away. However, it is important that the child be checked for stomach or intestinal disorders first.

Toilet Training

For children ages two to four:
Graham, Joan. *No More Diapers*. New York: Delacorte Press, 1971.
    Fiction.
        This story shows the child starting with a potty chair, taking responsibility for emptying it, and learning to like feeling dry and being positively reinforced by the parents.

For children ages four to eight:
Fassler, Joan. *Don't Worry Dear*. New York: Behavioral Publications, Inc., 1971. Fiction.

This book emphasizes that supportive parents give a young child freedom to outgrow her bed–wetting at her own rate.

For adults:

Fraiberg, Selma. *The Magic Years.* New York: Scribner's Sons, 1959. Nonfiction.

This book describes child development and how parents can make the most of their children's preschool years. The author offers several suggestions on toilet training.

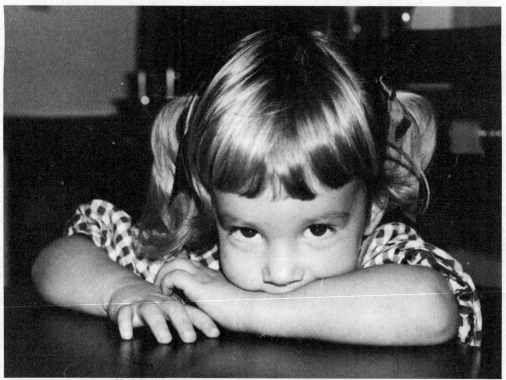

Children understand us at a very early age and deserve to be given honest answers.

Chapter Two

Eating Habits

Problems involving food are common in many households. This is unfortunate because they are so unnecessary. Many parents are concerned that their children are receiving a balanced diet. The child will only want cereal, crackers, and peanut butter or cheese, cereal, and raisins. Many times, there is so much discussion about food that the child comes to feel very important because of his different food habits. The more said about it, the more obstinate the child becomes, and the longer his idiosyncracy lasts.

It has been my experience that the best way to move a child through a stage like this, is of course, first to have him checked by a doctor and make sure that he is healthy. Then, if he seems to have plenty of energy and sleeps well at night, decide to ignore his eating habits.

While you are preparing dinner, you might ask him if he wants some of what the family will be eating. If he says, "No," don't prepare any for him. Let him get his own food together. Later, if he wants what you have prepared, let him taste it but say that you really don't have enough for him. (He will probably request some the next time.)

Be casual. Assume that as he grows and matures, he will cultivate the taste for other foods. Convey that message to him.

If your child's cravings include junk food, the best way to help is to eliminate these kinds of foods from your grocery shopping list. If they are not available, the child will be forced to make better choices.

The Fussy Eater

The family, including three teenagers, was together for dinner for a change, which pleased their father, Bill. He told them how happy he was to see them all getting a well-balanced meal. When the food was passed, he noticed that Jean did not take any potatoes, Bob passed on the green beans and Amy refused the meat.

"Now look here. I won't have this. I want to see all of you eat some of everything."

Bill proceeded to serve their plates with the foods that were missing. The children protested, saying that they did not want what he had given them. This made him more determined, and he said that they were not leaving the table until they had cleaned their plates.

The atmosphere was strained and no one enjoyed the family dinner. When Bill finished eating, he left the table and ordered the children not to get up until they had eaten every bite of their dinner.

As soon as he was gone, they found a way to "beat the system": Jean gave her potatoes to Amy, Amy gave her meat to Bob, and Bob gave his green beans to Jean. Then they cleaned their plates. When Bill came back to check on them, he praised the children for their obedience and reminded them how good it made him feel to see them eat a "well balanced" meal.

When parents spend so much energy on such unnecessary issues, they do not have enough left for the important matters. Children are forced to invent ways to "beat the system" and win the battles. Bill should realize that what the children eat is their business and that trying to force foods on them usually backfires and causes greater problems.

Chaotic Mealtimes

The majority of feeding problems arise because of some sort of psychological pressure placed on the child that is in conflict with his simple hunger needs. Overanxious adults have the mistaken notion that they know the child's hunger better than he does and that they must determine both the amount and the selection of food he eats. When children are expected or forced to eat despite the absence of hunger, eating problems arise. Some parents convey subtle messages, such as: "If you love me, you will eat," or "If you are sad, then you should eat," or "If you are happy, you should eat," or "If you are in trouble, you should eat." Others make the mistake of urging, begging, promising rewards (dessert), tricking, or force-feeding in an effort to get the child to eat what the parent thinks he should.

Clara Davis, in a classic research experiment, allowed children to select their own preferences and amounts from a variety of nutritious foods. She found that the children ate eagerly in astonishingly large quantities and then stopped abruptly. At the end of the experiment, the overall physical condition, digestion, and appetites of these children were well above average. Over a period of six months, despite erratic eating patterns, all the children eventually selected well-balanced diets. Somehow they were aware, even at an early age, of their own nutritional needs.

Scientists are now telling us that, if we overfeed babies, we will encourage a speed up in fat cell production, and that these extra fat cells stay in a person's body for life. They found that two-year-old children who were obese babies had twice the number of fat cells as those who were normal sized babies; five-year-old obese children had twice the number of fat cells as normal sized adults.

Here are some ways parents can help their children avoid eating problems:

- Provide well-balanced, colorful meals. (Don't fix special foods for individual family members.)

- Let your child select his own portions.

- Don't use meal time as a time for lecturing, complaining, reprimanding, and scolding. Make meal time pleasant with interesting conversations involving everyone.

- Don't reward your child for eating.

- Let your child know that eating is to satisfy hunger, not parents.

- If your child is not interested in meals but only in snacks, cut out the snacks for awhile and allow him to get hungry enough to want his meals.

- Be unconcerned about food jags. They usually run their course.

- Help your child to realize how his eating affects his overall disposition and health. For example, if he eats too many sweets, he feels sick, sluggish, and/or grumpy.

- Don't feel responsible for what your child eats. Provide nourishing foods and let him know as early as possible that his body is his responsibility, and the better he takes care of it, the better he will feel.

Weight Problems

Randall's father was reading the paper in the den when he heard the refrigerator door open.

"No, son, don't eat anything before dinner. The casserole in the refrigerator is for dinner. Close the door."

Not hearing the door close he called again, "I said 'close the door.' "

When eleven-year-old Randall came into the den a few minutes later his father could tell that he had been eating something.

"Did you eat that casserole?" Randall shook his head.

"What *did* you eat then? I can tell you ate something."

"Just some cookies—only a few."

"How many? I told you not to eat."

"Not many. I was hungry."

"I'm going to have to start locking up the food around here. You eat all the time. You sneak behind my back and eat leftovers, desserts, and snacks I bought for our lunches. And you're too fat anyway. You need to cut down on your food. You're going to be in real trouble when you hit the teens and no girl will look at you because you're too fat."

Randall didn't respond.

Later, when his father went into his bedroom to make a phone call, Randall went to the kitchen and finished off the cookies.

Randall's father is trying all the ways of discipline that don't work: shaming ("No girl will look at you"); ordering ("Don't eat anything. Close the refrigerator door"); threatening ("I'm going to lock up the food"); judging ("You're too fat, anyway") and questioning ("Did you eat the casserole?" "What *did* you eat?" "How many cookies?")

If his son is really overweight, this problem deserves more attention and careful handling than it is getting.

Randall's father is putting himself in charge of whether or not his son eats and when and what he eats. By doing so, he is assuming that Randall is not capable of regulating his own eating habits. When parents give unsolicited advice, they are increasing the probability that their children will delay learning survival skills and will come to depend on (and resent) others who make decisions for them.

Eating can be a very emotional issue. When parents get overly involved, the problem becomes intensified instead of solved.

Constructive alternatives might have been: discussing the matter with Randall; helping him choose healthy snacks; spending time with him (talking or playing); showing an interest in the child, not just in what he is eating; and demonstrating good eating habits himself.

Childhood
Stress

35

Bettina had brought her son, Todd, 13, to the health club to help him lose some weight. They had both received instructions and were using the equipment independently.

Bettina kept watching Todd.

"Now do it right, Todd. Being lazy won't help you lose weight. Since you are determined to eat enough for two, the only hope is exercise. That's not right. How many repetitions have you done?"

"Ten."

"You have not. I know you haven't done more than five. Now count. If you cheat, it won't do you any good. Do I have to show you how to work every machine?"

"I can do it, Mom. You just do your own stuff. I've done more than you have."

"That's a lie. Either do it right or don't do it at all."

"I hate this stuff."

"If I have to speak to you one more time, I'm taking you home."

Receiving no response from Todd, Bettina started in again. "Now don't do that. That's not the way he said to do it. Do you hear? Do I have to stop my workout to help you?"

She kept fussing and Todd continued his half-hearted attempts, putting forth little energy or effort on the workout. Finally, she muttered something about a waste of time and money and announced that they were leaving.

This mother had taken on the responsibility of helping her son shape up and lose weight. Rarely does this work.

The teen years are hard at best, and the last thing a child needs is to have a parent hassling him about his weight. This would probably be counterproductive, making a child more determined to "eat as much as he wants," "exercise when he wants," and do it "the way he wants."

Few boys thirteen years old would respond favorably to a mother trying to direct an exercise program.

At this age, it would be better if Bettina could have talked with her son and tried to interest him in some form of exercise. If he chose a health club, she might take him there and turn him over to an instructor whose job it is to teach the use of the equipment. She could agree to come back and pick Todd up at a certain time.

Bettina would be wise to find other people (preferably males) for her son to learn from, look up to, and emulate. Then perhaps he would be enthusiastic about an exercise program, wanting to feel proud and model the other people around him, instead of feeling that he is exercising for his mother. The chances for success are much better if he enters into an exercise program for the right reason, because *he* is motivated to get in shape.

A person has to be motivated from within to lose weight. Parents can be most helpful by accepting the child as he is, not nagging or becoming a policeman, and presenting a good model themselves for proper diet and exercise. Weight belongs to the owner and the control of it is up to him.

Serious Nutritional Diseases

In this decade, much attention has been given to anorexia nervosa and bulimia. Even though historical medical records show that they are not new disorders, they have never before been so prevalent as they are today. It is estimated that one in every one hundred teenage girls and young women will be affected by anorexia, and one out of five college-age females will become bulimic. Nine out of ten cases of these eating disorders occur in women.

The problem cuts across racial, socioeconomic, and intellectual boundaries. It can begin as early as age seven and can reach well into the adult years. Although medical causes should not be ruled out entirely, social and psychological factors are most often found to be at the root of the problem, especially parental and sibling relationships.

Persons affected by eating disorders report feelings of isolation and failure. Many are actually high achievers who are never satisfied with accomplishment but rather strive for perfection.

The most susceptible times in a person's life are: before or after puberty, a move, a parental divorce, death of a loved one, or after a disappointing love relationship.

Symptoms of anorexia nervosa include:

- loss of twenty percent of body weight
- obsession with weight loss, thinness, and food
- intense fear of weight gain and obesity
- social isolation and withdrawal
- compulsive exercising
- loss of menstrual periods
- denial of problems.

Symptoms of bulimia include:

- secretive eating binges unrelated to hunger and enormous intake of high-calorie foods
- binges occurring from several a week to many every day
- vomiting, use of diet pills, laxatives, and/or diuretics
- shame, guilt, and remorse
- fatigue and weakness
- intense concern with weight, appearance, and opinion of others
- menstrual irregularities.

If anorexia or bulimia is diagnosed, it is necessary to seek treatment. The best approach is a combination of medical attention, psychotherapy, and nutritional counseling for the patient as well as counseling for the other family members. Self-help groups are often effective in addition to the medical and psychotherapeutic treatment.

These national organizations provide information on anorexia and bulimia and can provide information on a local level:

American Anorexia/Bulimia Association, Inc.
133 Cedar Lane
Teaneck, NJ 07666
(201) 836-1800

Anorexia Nervosa and Related Eating Disorders, Inc.
P.O. Box 5102
Eugene, OR 97405
(503) 344-1144

National Anorexic Aid Society, Inc.
P.O. Box 29461
Columbus, OH 43229
(614) 846-2588

National Association of Anorexia Nervosa and Associated
Disorders
P.O. Box 271
Highland Park, IL 60035
(312) 837-3438

Eating Disorders

For children ages 4 to 8:
Hoban, Russell C. *Bread and Jam for Frances*. New York: Harper and
Row Publishers, 1964. Fiction.
Frances, a little badger, refuses to eat anything other than
bread and jam. Her parents help her widen her food
preferences.

For children ages 8 to 12:
Holland, Isabelle. *Dinah and the Green Fat Kingdom*. New York: J. B.
Lippincott Co., 1978. Fiction.
An overweight young girl wrestles out from under her
feelings of being able to do nothing right.

For children ages 12 to 16:

Van Leeuwen, Jean. *I Was A 98-Pound Duckling*. New York: Dial
 Press Inc., 1972. Fiction.

 This story humorously describes the problems of an
 adolescent girl who feels she is a hopeless mess.

For adults:

Landau, Elaine. *Why Are They Starving Themselves?* New York: Julian
 Messner, 1983. Nonfiction.

 This book gives a thorough and compassionate overview of
 eating disorders. The author includes personal vignettes and
 valuable suggestions to help potential victims.

Whitener, Carole B. and Marie H. Keeling. *Nutrition Education for
 Young Children*. Englewood Cliffs, NJ: Prentice-Hall, 1984.
 Nonfiction.

 This book offers "hands on" learning activities designed to
 help young children develop good basic eating habits.

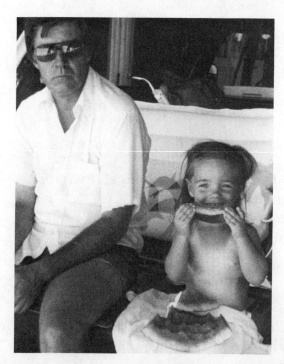

*You can help your child by
eliminating junk food from
your shopping list.*

Chapter Three

Siblings

All parents hope and believe that their children love each other and want to be in each other's company. Most of us deny the fact that no child would actually choose to share his parents' love and attention, and because of that, at times all older children would like to do away with (or send back) the little intruder.

If parents understand the problems siblings face, then there are many things they can do to help their children grow to love and respect each other. They can make each position in the family advantageous and help every child to feel important, significant, and irreplaceable.

Without wisdom and careful handling, however, the arguing, bickering, fighting, jealousy, and rivalry between brothers and sisters can get out of hand and become a debilitating force within the family. The continuous unpleasantness, strife, and grief that become a daily diet for a child while he is young can be carried with him into adulthood and diminish his chances of ever entering into peaceful and mutually satisfying relationships.

The New Baby

Claire's mother was expecting her second child. She and her husband had taken two-year-old Claire to her grandmother's house in a nearby city the week before the baby was due to be sure they wouldn't get caught at the last minute. Claire and her parents spent the night at her grandmother's, but her parents left early the next morning before Claire was awake.

When Claire awoke, she called for her mommy. Her grandmother went into the room and told her that her parents had gone home to get a new baby. They would be back to pick her up in a few weeks.

Claire was frantic. She whined and cried for her mother off and on all day. Her grandmother tried everything she knew to console her. She rocked, read and sang to her, then took her outside for a walk. Nothing distracted her for long. She kept begging for her mother.

At first, her crying was loud and demanding. After a few days, though, Claire became sullen and quiet. Her face was sad and no one seemed able to cheer her up. When she cried, she cried softly to herself.

By the time her parents came to pick her up two-and-a-half weeks later, their once bright-eyed and happy child seemed uninterested and apathetic. She showed no interest in the baby and not much more in her parents.

When parents know they are going to leave their child, they need to spend time beforehand preparing her for the separation. Even with children as young as Claire, it is important to tell them ahead of time and in as many ways as you can about the upcoming event. You might write a little illustrated book using the child's name, telling exactly what is going to happen, why the mother is going to the hospital, where the child will be staying, and some of the things to look forward to: her grandmother is going to take her to the zoo; they will bake cookies;

she will help to feed the dog; she will receive calls, cards, and presents from her parents.

Suggest that she choose something special that belongs to her parents to take with her.

You might write postcards ahead of time and arrange to have them mailed so that the child will receive them daily. Buy and wrap a small inexpensive present for each day and take them to the relative's house to dispense each morning at breakfast. After dinner each night, it might be helpful to call her on the phone and talk with her to give her something to look forward to and to keep you very alive to her. Always reassure her that you will be coming to get her as soon as possible and let her know that you love and miss her.

When children have to deal with surprises and sudden changes, they become fearful and anxious, not knowing when another unplanned event will take place and change their world. This often destroys trust.

When you are back home together again, expect some displays of anger and hostility. Your firstborn needs extra attention and understanding.

Friends who want to be helpful can offer to keep the new baby for you, to give you a chance to spend some uninterrupted time with the older child. They would also be wise to bring a gift to the older child instead of the new baby when they come to visit. It is much more needed by the child who has been temporarily pushed out.

Remember that this is a difficult time for a child, having first to adjust to the separation and then to the new baby. However, good planning, preparation, and sympathetic understanding will minimize the long-term detrimental effects.

> Elizabeth was carrying her baby on her shoulder and pushing the grocery cart. Ricky, 3, obviously unhappy, was walking around the store, tugging on her coat and begging to be picked up. His mother was distracted and ignored Ricky at first and, when he persisted, told him to go away. She said, "You are so bad that I don't want to have anything to do with you. Look at

your little sister. She is so good. You don't hear her crying and whining, do you? Why can't you be good like her? Just go away. I'm tired of looking at you."

Elizabeth's sharp words to her son made him more upset. His whining turned to loud crying and the three of them created an unpleasant scene in the grocery store. By the time they checked out, Elizabeth had spanked Ricky, and he had collapsed in the middle of the floor, screaming.

This was an almost impossible predicament for Elizabeth to create for herself. It is better, if at all possible, to leave the baby with a friend or relative and take the toddler to the store. This gives the mother a chance to spend some time alone with her oldest when he would not have to compete with his new little sister. Naturally, being jealous and tired, he wanted the same attention his mother was giving to the baby. She made the matter worse by comparing his behavior to that of his sister. Unfortunately, this makes him dislike the baby more, and he will probably have a further need to demonstrate his frustrations (by hurting, withdrawing, or misbehaving). Parents should be very careful to avoid such comparisons.

(If Elizabeth had had no choice but to take both children to the store, she could have provided an infant seat in the grocery cart for the baby, encouraged the toddler to help her select food for lunch, and/or promised a special treat when they finished shopping if he could cooperate.)

Dr. Lee Salk says that, in some ways, having a new baby arrive on the scene is "an irreversible tragedy" for the older child who has now been shoved out of his "number one" position. There are definitely no immediate gains for him brought about by the arrival of this intruder, and we should not fool ourselves into thinking that he will, anytime soon, "love" his new little brother or sister.

The way that this traumatic time is dealt with will, to a great extent, determine the feelings that our children will later develop for each other and the intensity of the sibling rivalry that will exist in the home. Being aware that this is a difficult time is the first step toward making the transition tolerable and not permanently damaging.

Below are some ways parents can help older children cope with the arrival of a new baby:

- Prepare the child ahead of time by telling him about the new event. Don't tell him so soon that he will tire of waiting, but in plenty of time for him to prepare mentally himself for the changes that will take place. Admit the negative effects as well as the positive, e.g., the new baby may cry a lot and may take much of the parents' time. Sometimes, the child might even wish the baby could be given away. Assure him that you will still love him as much as ever and that you will continue to have special times together.

- Be sure that your child understands that Mother is going to be away for a few days to have the new baby but will soon return. It is ideal if he can visit her and the new baby and see that mother is okay, can smile and laugh, and has not changed in any way. If this is not possible, she could phone every day or might leave small daily presents to help tide him over until she can return.

- Be careful not to overdo the enthusiasm for the new baby when you return home. Spend time alone with the older child and be sure that special attention is given to him by visitors, relatives, and other family members.

- Don't "farm out" the older child unless absolutely necessary. This will increase his feelings of being pushed out and abandoned.

- Expect and accept regression of the older child. He may suck his thumb, want a bottle, demand to be rocked, or need to return to diapers. Let him be a baby again, if he wants to. This will be temporary and short-lived if his needs are accepted and if he is not shamed for them.

- Make him feel important. Show him pictures and talk about when he was a baby. Help him to see the advantages of being grown-up. ("You can stay up later, tie your own shoes, eat at the table with the grown-ups, talk instead of cry, and walk and run instead of lying in a crib.")

- Let him help with the baby, if he wants to, but don't force him to feel responsible.

- Allow him to express his negative feelings. Don't tell him that he loves his baby sister or tell others in front of him that he loves her. This may cause him to feel guilty, since that is not the word for what he feels much of the time. Remember, no matter how much we *want* our children to love each other, their feelings are ambivalent, at best, and they need time to sort them out and an atmosphere where they can be safely expressed and nurtured.

The existence of these potential problems should not keep parents from having a second child. When trying to decide when and if to plan for another baby, I feel that the most important consideration should be how well you are satisfied with your first child, your parenting, and the strength of the bonds of love which now exist between you and your spouse. Although making a decision to have another child is costly, making a decision *not* to have another one could leave you with a high or higher price to pay.

Rivalry

While they were waiting to be served at a restaurant, Greg, 8, and Don, 5, were amusing themselves by coloring on the paper place mats that had been provided for this purpose. Soon, they began to argue over who was going to use the blue crayon. Don hit Greg and tried to grab the crayon out of his hand.

Tony, who had not been paying attention to what his boys were doing, became annoyed when they began to fight. He turned to them and asked who had hit whom and who started it. Because he got conflicting stories, he took the crayon from Greg and gave it to Don. The little boy snickered and appeared to be quite pleased as he watched his brother tear up his place mat and throw it on the floor.

When parents attempt to settle differences between their children, they often cause more problems than they solve. They frequently reward the culprit and punish the innocent one. At any rate, their intervention and attention encourages children to continue fighting. It is best to stay out of children's fights. If this is not possible (as in a public place), they might offer an incentive for cooperative behavior or take the crayon away from both of them and give it back when they have come up with a solution to the problem. This puts the responsibility for settling their differences where it belongs, squarely on the shoulders of those involved.

Experts tell us that the place a child has in the family constellation will be an important determinant of his or her personality development.

All of us have been greatly influenced by those people who surround us in our early years, particularly our closest family members. The adaptation we make to those people to a large extent determines our adult interactions with our peers, our marriage partners, our supervisors, and the people who work for us. These relationships can be very rewarding or they can be a constant source of irritation, depending on the way we related to those around us when we were very young.

Although there are many exceptions, some of the research findings indicate that:

- First-born and only children are more responsible, more often chosen as leaders, more competitive, score higher on achievement tests, hold more eminent positions, talk sooner and better, and have more baby pictures taken of them.

- Middle children have more relaxed parents, tend to be less concerned about winning approval, feel squeezed out, often try to be "different" from the oldest, and are more outgoing and more popular.

- Youngest children have the highest sociability ratings of all. They tend to be easygoing and "charming" and are sometimes labeled as "rebels." They are the most "made much of" and "picked on," and they are masters at letting other people "do the work."

- Girls with brothers and no sisters tend to be very feminine.

- Girls with one older brother tend to be more aggressive and dominant.

- Boys with one older sister tend to be more passive.

- Two sisters close together tend to be very feminine.

- Two brothers close together tend to be very masculine.

- Older brothers of boys tend to be leaders and to get along well with males.

- Younger brothers of sisters tend to get along better with girls and will look for wives who will wait on them hand and foot.

It is important to remember that these are simply observations and the effect that they will have on the children born into these positions will be determined both by the perception each child receives of his own situation and the way he is treated by other family members.

> It was Jimmy's first day of school. His parents had gone to great lengths to prepare for the big event. They had bought him new clothes, shoes, lunchbox, pencils, and pencil case. He had been taken to see his new school and to meet his teacher. They had gotten up early and taken movies of each event—getting dressed, eating breakfast, walking out the door, boarding the school bus.

> His mother cried a little as the bus rounded the corner out of sight. She and his father walked back to the house slowly, talking about how cute Jimmy was and how fast he had grown up.

When they got back to the house, the mother went upstairs to wake up four-year-old Billy. He was not in his room. She called but got no answer. She looked around for him and asked her husband to help. He looked in the garage and found Billy sitting on the floor, in the midst of tires, pedals, fenders, and bicycle parts. He had taken his bike apart and was pounding on the fenders with a hammer.

Billy's father called to his wife, "Here he is, Lillian, making a mess in the garage."

To Billy, he said, angrily, "What do you think you're doing—ruining your bicycle? Boy, why do you have to take everything apart? Why, look at Jimmy's bike. It is all shiny and clean. Why can't you be like him? He takes good care of his things and you ruin everything you can get your hands on. You'll never be ready for school. I don't know what they are going to do with you when they get *you*. They won't know what hit them. Get in here. Go to your room—and stay there—until I say you can come out."

The father went back in the house to eat breakfast. Billy got up slowly. As he walked by Jimmy's bike, he kicked it with his foot and knocked it off the kick stand.

Billy had watched Jimmy get much attention during the past several days, and his jealousy got the best of him. This is not at all unusual. Parents need to be aware of the feelings between children and take care not to add to the problems that naturally exist.

If treated carefully, sibling rivalry—the competition of brothers and sisters for the love and attention of their parents—is mild and can be outgrown. If it is mishandled or aggravated, it can spill over into peer competition for friends, grades and sports.

Psychiatrists say that twenty-five percent of us carry sibling rivalry into our adulthood, like excess baggage. It surfaces as competition for the limelight, jealousy with our colleagues, inability to share those we love with others.

The messages we give our children come back to us loud and clear. If one child is viewed as "perfect," another child may try to excel in "imperfection."

Parents can minimize sibling rivalry, by:

- avoiding comparisons
- allowing children to argue, disagree, and work out compromises (If it becomes unbearable, put a distance between parents and children.)
- building on each child's strengths and encouraging each to excel in different areas
- making each child feel special and valued and helping him to be glad he is different

The mistake most parents make is to try to treat each child the same way. This makes children more competitive. When we realize our children are different people with different needs and wants, different body rhythms, temperaments, and personalities, life will be smoother. In other words, reinforce your children's "differentness" and help them focus on ways of making each child unique and special.

Growing up with siblings can be beneficial. With careful handling, brothers and sisters can learn to depend on each other, share with each other, and help one another. Ideally, they can develop a strong sense of family and cooperation which will be a valuable asset as they grow older and need the support and skills necessary to get along in the adult world.

> Susan called the children to go with her to pick up cleaning and to get a birthday present. As they came to the car, Tina, 7, was crying, saying that Tony, 9, had hit her. Susan said, "Tony, you know better than to hit your little sister." Tony started to defend himself, and the fight was on.

> Susan lost her temper and spent the ten minutes it took to drive to the mall yelling at her children.

Susan got a splitting headache and felt guilty for yelling at her children. They laid down in the back seat of the car and got very quiet.

These children were accustomed to getting their mother's attention when they fought.

Without realizing it, many parents actually train their children to argue, bicker, and pick on each other. One child provokes another child into an overt aggressive act. The second child is blamed and may be punished. The first child has actually been rewarded for being the instigator of the problem. This leads to resentment on the part of the punished child who will most likely begin to devise a way to retaliate.

By interfering or intervening, parents are inadvertently teaching their children that "it pays to fight."

We need to somehow reverse this procedure and teach our children that "it pays to get along." The best way to do this is to ignore children's squabbles, and, instead, reward their cooperative behavior.

Susan could have said, "If you will ride all the way to the mall with me with no fighting, hitting or name-calling, I will give you a surprise when we get home. If either of you fights, no matter who started it or whose fault it is, neither of you will receive the surprise. Understand?"

Parents need to step out of conflicts and give the children room to work things out. If you are in a crowded space (a car), try to withdraw mentally from the conflict (refuse to react, turn on the radio, sing to yourself, or pull off the road and stop, saying nothing). You will find that the fighting will diminish rapidly because your children will learn that it doesn't pay off.

When left alone to settle their differences, children establish far more fair and equal relationships than we can provide for them.

Donnie, 12, had been in the den alone watching T.V. when Marie, 14, came in from school. She hurried into the house and announced that she wanted to watch her soap opera. She changed the channel, which infuriated Donnie. He got up quickly and changed it back to the channel he was watching. A verbal fight broke out between them.

Their mother, hearing the noise, hurried into the den, saying, "Your fighting drives me crazy. Marie, Donnie was here first. What makes you think you have the right to come in and change the channel he was watching? That's not fair. First come, first served." Marie protested that she couldn't help it that Donnie got home from school before she did, and she didn't think it was fair for him to always get his way. Finally she ran out of the room, up the stairs, and slammed her door.

This kind of exchange goes on in every home, and parents need to know how to handle it. The children need to be taught that the privilege of watching T.V. is earned by cooperative behavior. If they cannot work out agreeable solutions, then the T.V. is turned off. When children understand that they are responsible for solving these kinds of problems, they often work out elaborate solutions and become very adept at learning to negotiate and cooperate. Parents begin to like their children better, and parenthood becomes less difficult.

One of the great lessons that children learn from their interactions with their siblings is that human conflicts, though sometimes very intense and painful, are inevitable but tolerable, and can be worked out. Through them we can learn the important lessons of dialogue, compromise, debate and negotiation, strengths we will need in later life.

Sibling Rivalries

For children ages 4 to 8:
Alexander, Martha G. *Nobody Asked Me if I Wanted a Baby Sister*. New York: The Dial Press, 1971. Fiction.
    A little boy cannot stand the fuss over his new baby sister. Young children can easily identify with his predicament.

Stein, Sara Bonnett. *That New Baby: An Open Family Book for Parents and Children Together*. New York: Walker and Co., 1974. Nonfiction.

This book describes the different feelings that young children might have before and after a new baby enters the family. An accompanying adult text helps to handle questions brought up by the child.

Vigna, Judith. *Couldn't We Have a Turtle Instead*? Chicago: Albert Whitman and Co., 1975. Fiction.

A humorous story which describes a child's feelings about having a new baby in the family.

Viorst, Judith. *I'll Fix Anthony*. New York: Harper and Row Publishers, Inc., 1969. Fiction.

An older sibling's behavior toward his younger brother frustrates the little one, who then relieves his frustration through his imagination.

For children ages 8 to 12:

Armer, Alberta. *Screwball*. Cleveland, OH: William Collins and World Publishers, 1963. Fiction.

Twin boys struggle for acceptance and friendship. The characterizations are outstanding.

Blume, Judy. *Tales of a Fourth Grade Nothing*. New York: E. P. Dutton and Co., 1972. Fiction.

A humorous description of a fourth-grade boy's difficulties with a little brother.

Child Study Association of America. *Brothers and Sisters Are Like That! Stories to Read to Yourself*. New York: Thomas Y. Cromell, Co., 1971. Fiction.

This is a collection of ten short stories on the theme of sibling relationships.

Cleary, Beverly. *Beezuz and Ramona*. West Caldwell, NJ: William Morrow and Co., 1955. Fiction.

Two sisters share the problems and joys of being in the same family.

Greene, Constance Clarke. *I and Sproggy*. New York: The Viking Press, Inc., 1978. Fiction.

This amusing book describes the changing relationship between a stepbrother and his stepsister.

For adults:

Dreikurs, Rudolph and Vicki Soltz. *Children: The Challenge*. New York: Hawthorn Books, 1964. Nonfiction.

This book proposes ways to handle children by recognizing the goals behind their actions.

Gordon, Thomas. *Parent Effectiveness Training*. New York: Peter H. Wyden, 1970. Nonfiction.

This book presents a complete theoretical system for better understanding of the parent-child relationship.

Kersey, Katharine. *Sensitive Parenting*. Washington, D.C.: Acropolis Books, Ltd., 1983. Nonfiction.

This book explains how parents can give their children the love, discipline, and independence they need.

With careful handling, brothers and sisters can learn to depend on each other and share with each other.

Chapter Four

School

Ideally, we want our children to become lifetime learners, to be curious, ask questions, search for answers, and read books well beyond the time when they are required to do so.

Unfortunately, however, for many children the school experience is so painful that they equate "learning" with "school" and, early on, give up on both. This can happen when parents are not ready or able to let go of their child, to let him grow up, or consider what is best for him.

It is up to the parent to make certain that the child finds his best "learning match"—the best environment for *him*—where he is stimulated, excited, and motivated to grow and learn. It is the parent's responsibility to be sure that the school fits the child and not try to re-form the child to fit the school.

Often the personality of the teacher and the child do not fit. Sometimes the child is over his head, not ready for the material which he is expected to master. Other times, the child is not adequately challenged; he is being given work that he mastered a year ago. This child develops the notion that schools and teachers are dumb, and he uses his energies to figure ways to beat the system.

Frequently, highly motivated and perfectionist parents unconsciously convey to the child that they expect him to be perfect. Having been raised on the "When a job is once begun, never leave it 'til it's done. Be the labor, great or small, do it well or not at all" philosophy, they do not realize what an impossible burden they place on their child. Understandably, they worry when he cries if he makes a mistake of falls apart when he can't do something, and they wonder why he is so hard on himself.

Unless there are other signs of trouble (sleepless nights, regression, acting out behavior, restlessness, or reluctance to go to school), parents are wiser to look for outside interests of their own and leave what goes on at school up to those who are trained to make educational decisions.

Parents need to be able to determine what is the best learning environment is for their child and seek diligently until they find the best placement for him.

School Problems

Louise decided to go back to work and to leave her little girl at a nearby day-care center. She checked out the center and felt that the environment was one she would want for her child.

The first day, Louise got up early, made all the preparations, and had Mary Lou there when the center opened. She went inside with her to make sure that she was settled and happy.

After a few minutes, Louise felt it was time for her to leave.

"Come here, Mary Lou, and give me a kiss. Here, give me a hug too. You won't see me all day, so give me two kisses."

Mary Lou started to cry.

"Oh, what's wrong? Why are you crying? Do you want me to stay for just another minute? All right. Come over here and look at the nice toys. Do you see one you want to play with? Here is a nice little baby doll. Want to play with her while I am gone?"

Mary Lou grabbed hold of her mother's dress.

"Oh dear, how can I leave now?" Louise thought.

"Come on, Mary Lou, please let go of my dress. I'll bring you some candy when I come back to get you. Please let go. I have to go to work."

Finally, one of the day–care workers offered to pick Mary Lou up and get her interested in playing with the other children.

Louise left reluctantly, still hearing the sobbing of her daughter.

As soon as she was gone, Mary Lou stopped crying.

Some mothers have a very hard time leaving their children—often out of feelings of guilt—and the children sense their hesitation. These children usually have an equally hard time making the separation. Louise needs to see that it would be in the best interests of the child for her to be more sure of herself and leave her daughter with a matter-of-fact attitude. It sometimes helps if the mother lets the child keep something of hers (an old glove, nightgown, or pocketbook). She should also remind the child that she will be back at a certain time and give her something to look forward to upon her return, such as stopping at the park or ice cream store on the way home. The parent should always tell the child ahead of time when she will be leaving, and then follow through without hesitation. Usually, as the parent becomes more confident, so does her child.

Jesse, 5, had taken his shoes off for story time, the last activity of the day. When it was over, the children usually went outdoors to play until their parents came to pick them up.

The teacher asked Jesse to put his shoes on by himself, something she knew he could to. The child ignored her request.

When the children lined up to go outside, Jesse lined up with them. The teacher reminded him that when he had put his shoes on, he could come outside to wait for his mother. The other children left with the teacher and Jesse stayed behind with the aide.

When Jesse's mother arrived, the teacher told her the situation, and asked her to wait outside until Jesse had obeyed the teacher's request. Instead, Jesse's mother hurried into the building, saying, "My poor baby. I'll help him put his shoes on."

When she reached the classroom her son already had one shoe on and practically tied. She took the remaining shoe, cooing, "My poor baby." Jesse objected, telling his mom that he could do it himself. He started crying, saying that he wanted to do it, so that he could go out to play with the other children.

Jesse's mother ignored her son and finished the job, trying to soothe him with "Now, now, everything is all right. You can stop crying. Mommy has put your shoes on. Now you can go out to play."

Jesse stopped crying, jumped up and ran outside. "Teacher, Mommy put my shoes on. Now I can play!"

Jesse's mother undermined the teacher's request, teaching her son that he did not have to obey the teacher once she had arrived. She reinforced the child's dependency and inadequacy by doing for him what he knew he could and should have done for himself. She showed insensitivity to the child and disrespect for the teacher.

It is often difficult for parents to let their children suffer the consequences of their actions. In an effort to keep them from hurting, they also stifle their growth and independence.

Children should be encouraged to obey their teachers. If parents disagree with the teacher's methods, they need to speak privately to her, not contradict her requests and tell the child he does not have to obey her.

Our goal with children is to help them grow out of their need for us and into self-sufficient, dependable, competent adults; the time to start this process is while they are still young.

When we overdo and over protect, we are telling the child he is helpless, and eventually he will live up to that expectation. He will stop trying to be independent and, instead, let us take charge of his life for him. He will expect us to watch out for him, protect him from danger, and get him out of any scrapes he might get into. As he matures physically, his emotional maturity will fall behind, and when the time comes for him to take full responsibility for his life, he will not be prepared to do so. Such children become irresponsible spouses and disgruntled adults.

It is a disservice to the child to undermine the educational system of which he is a part. This makes him lose respect for his teachers and fellow classmates and may eventually cause him to lose interest in his work.

Nothing discourages teachers faster than parents who constantly challenge them and undermine their efforts. Teachers, like the rest of us, need to be respected and trusted in their judgment. There is much more to education than pushing children as far and fast as they can go.

Parents and teachers share a common concern, the education of the child. The more they support one another, the better it will be for the child. If they pull against each other, it will be the child who suffers.

Parents need to involve themselves as much as possible in the child's school life, but in a *supportive* role. They should make every effort to get to know the child's teacher, principal, friends, and school policies. If possible, they should attend Open House, volunteer in the classroom, participate in the P.T.A., accompany the class on trips, and support their activities.

> Linda had called four times for six-year-old Lisa to get up. The fifth time, she went to the child's room and pulled back the covers. "Lisa, get up this minute. I'm tired of calling you. You'll be late for school. Now, hurry up."
>
> Lisa squirmed and reached for the covers, pulling them back up over her and saying nothing.
>
> "Come on, Lisa, I meant it," Linda said, yanking the covers off

once more. "Where are your clothes? Do you need me to dress you?" She took a dress from the closet and laid it on the bed.

"I don't want to wear that dress," said Lisa, sitting up. "I hate that dress—you know I hate that dress."

Slowly, Lisa stood up and went to her dresser. She started rummaging through her clothes and pulled out some pants and a shirt.

Linda left the room muttering, "Wear anything you want, even if they don't match. See if I care how you look."

A few minutes later, Linda called upstairs, "Lisa, your breakfast is getting cold and if you don't hurry you'll miss the bus."

Where's my other shoe? I can't find it anywhere."

"I'm sure I don't know," said Linda. "It's wherever you left it when you took it off. Now come on and eat breakfast. We'll look for the shoe after you eat."

"I don't want bacon. I hate bacon! Besides, this bacon is burned." Lisa picked up her bacon and threw it on the floor.

"Well, eat your egg and toast," said Linda, picking up the bacon and throwing it in the garbage can. Lisa ate a few bites of egg and toast.

"Come on, Lisa. I'll help you look for your other shoe." Linda left the room and started up the stairs. Lisa came slowly behind her. Looking under the bed and in the closet, Linda finally found the other shoe.

"Here, hurry up now. I'm sure it's time for the bus. Brush your teeth, quickly now! Here's your lunch money and your books. Don't forget your spelling notebook. Come on, Lisa, hurry."
"Honestly, this is a terrible way to start the day. Tonight you can go to bed early and maybe you'll feel more like getting up tomorrow."

Lisa grumbled as she picked up her books, "I don't want to go to school." She heard the bus coming down the street, and ran out the door to meet it.

Linda was exhausted from her daily ritual.

Many families go through such trials every morning when a parent assumes the responsibility for the child's behavior. Children are perfectly capable of getting themselves up, dressed, and ready for school, though many a well-meaning parent denies the child the dignity of assuming responsibility for herself. In the case above, Lisa knew that her mother would get her ready for school, and so allowed her to do so.

If Linda decided to change the daily ritual and make Lisa responsible for herself, it would be wise for them to first have a talk. Linda could explain to her daughter that she would no longer be responsible for getting her ready for school. Together they might buy an alarm clock and plan a way to select school clothes, maybe choosing them the night before. Then Linda could help Lisa make a chart with rewards for different tasks completed: getting up on time, getting dressed, eating breakfast, brushing teeth, collecting books and lunch money. She would get a point for each task completed by the time the kitchen timer went off. When she had accumulated a certain number of points, she would receive a reward—having a friend spend the night, a trip to the zoo, or lunch out with her mother.

When families implement such systems, all members feel better about themselves and have more energy to devote to positive interactions, which build—rather than destroy—self esteem.

> The children in the class had been told that they would be taking a reading test. They were warned to do their best, because if they did well, they would be moved up to a level higher in reading, but if they did poorly, they would be moved back with the slower readers.

Janie was panicked. As the test began, she tried to concentrate, but she found it difficult to keep her mind on her work. About half way through the test, she gave up. She put her pencil down, laid her head on her desk, and began to cry.

When Janie got home, she slung her books on the floor and started yelling at her mother.

"I hate school. It's not fair. I'm dumb. I'll probably fail the third grade. I'm just stupid, stupid, stupid. I knew the stuff on the test, but I was the slowest one in the class. I knew I would flunk anyway."

"What are you talking about, Janie? Tell me."

Her mother had just begun to ask questions when the phone rang. It was Janie's teacher. She called to let her know that Janie had been put back into the slower reading group.

The scenario above is very sad, yet one that is often repeated in our modern society. It is unfortunate that teachers are often forced, by outside pressure, to use every conceivable tactic to make children perform. Most of them know, deep down, that this does not produce happy, interested, motivated children.

Parents, because of their anxiety and concern, want their children to develop the skills that will enable them to compete for good education, better jobs, and higher salaries.

We need to recognize that children, by nature, are eager learners. When we try to bend the child to fit the expectations of the school or the parent, we often defeat our purpose altogether.

Even children who can excel often decide at some point that they no longer want to live to suit someone else. Those who can't live up to the expectations set for them give up early, like Janie. They put their heads down and cry. They often internalize shame, guilt, and failure.

If the child is not progressing well, the parents will see the first signs— the child will begin to wet the bed, bite his nails, complain of stomach aches and headaches, or have nightmares. It is up to the parents to do *something*. If they just let the situation get worse, the damage could be irreparable.

What can they do?

First, talk the situation over with the child. Encourage him to talk over the problem with the teacher, guidance counselor or principal. It may be that a simple change in schedule or seating could solve the problem.

If the child can't or won't tackle the problem, the parents need to help by interceding. Speak first to the teacher to see if the problem can be solved within the existing framework.

If the situation is not improved, the parents need to exercise their parental rights and God-given intuition to find a situation for the child which will be right for him. No child should be made to endure an intolerable situation.

We need to remember that there is no such thing as a child who can't learn. It is the parents' right to find the best placement for their child. Although it might take time to find the "right match," the effort is well worth it. The saddest thing that can happen to a child in school is for him to lose interest and confidence in his ability to learn. No one knows and understands the child as well as the parents. They can play an important role in making the education of their child rewarding, challenging, and successful.

There are many factors to think about when considering a change of schools for a child. His adjustment to the classroom is of utmost importance.

- Is he happy?
- Is he working hard?
- Does he feel good about himself and his ability to learn?

If the answers to these questions are positive, whether he is reading on the third or fourth grade level, whether he is introduced to decimals this year or next, will not matter in the long run. If he is eager to learn and introduced to new work when he has gained mastery of previous material, he will be motivated to stretch himself, and will arrive in his own time.

> Gloria, eight, was sitting at the breakfast table crying softly. She hadn't touched her food, and her mother was frustrated. "What's wrong, Gloria? Why aren't you eating? I fixed your favorite breakfast, and you haven't touched it. You'll be late for school. Hurry up. What's wrong with you?"
>
> Gloria kept on crying. "I can't eat. My stomach hurts. I don't want to go to school. I don't feel good."
>
> Her mother was perplexed. Feeling Gloria's warm head, she took her temperature and found that it was 99°. "Well I guess you'd better stay home, if you don't feel well. I hate for you to miss school, but I know you can't learn if you are sick. Go on back to bed. I'll call the doctor later."

There are many degrees of "school phobia," a disorder characterized by "an irrational fear of going to school." Some of the most extreme cases are accompanied by nausea, headaches, stomachache, diarrhea, paleness, weight loss, dizziness, and sleep disturbances. Frequently, the symptoms disappear on weekends and holidays.

School phobia is real and needs to be dealt with, not overlooked. Its causes are often complex and even the child himself cannot identify them. Sometimes, the fear can be traced to a particular event or situation: a harsh teacher, an unpleasant recess experience, a fearsome bus driver, a mean child, bullying boys at the bus stop, dressing out at phys. ed., failing a particular subject.

There are also problems at home which can cause children not to want to separate themselves from the family. Such events as illness, fights, divorce, separation, a new baby, or a move to a new neighborhood can cause children to become anxious about leaving home. One of the most common causes for school phobia is a dependent relationship between parent and child. If a mother is oversolicitous and tries to shield her child from all unpleasant experiences by anticipating and meeting his every need, the child "catches" her anxiety and is very unsure of his own ability to cope with "the world out there."

The treatment for school phobia is most effective if it is begun immediately after it is recognized. An examination by a physician is a good place to start. Once the child has received a clean bill of health, measures should be taken to uncover the cause. The child should be listened to and taken seriously. If something can be changed or altered—a different teacher, more careful supervision on the playground, a different placement in math—it should be taken care of as soon as possible. If the problem is complex and seems to involve unhealthy relationships between family members, outside help should be sought.

It is important to remember that authoritarian measures—force, coercion, shame, or physical punishment—will do more harm than good. Children who are stricken with school phobia need understanding, reassurance, support, praise, and recognition from home as well as from school.

School phobia is no disgrace. It can happen to any child, from any home in any school. It is a very real problem and needs our immediate attention.

Parental Expectations

Fred's mother had come to the parent teacher conference loaded with complaints. She threatened to take Fred, nine, out of school and place him in another school.

"Fred is not working up to his potential," she began. "I don't know why he is still on multiplication when he should be in decimals and fractions. His next door neighbor is the same age and goes to another school. He is way ahead of Fred. You just don't work him hard enough. He is basically lazy anyway and you don't motivate him to work up to his potential."

"Mrs. Madison, it would be useless to start Fred on decimals and fractions when he still needs to master multiplication. He does *not* know his multiplication facts and would be lost if I moved him on to more complicated arithmetic."

"He *does* know his multiplication tables. If he gets mixed up at school, that's your fault. There are too many distractions in your classroom, and he just can't concentrate. That is one more reason why I should take him out of this school.

"Here, Mrs. Madison, let me show you his work today. If he brings his papers home to you the way he is supposed to, you already have seen the kind of work he does in school and the trouble he has with multiplication facts." The teacher got out some of Fred's work to show his mother.

"Well, I haven't seen work this bad. That's funny—he knows this at home and forgets it when he gets to school. I think he is too busy playing and having fun here to get his work done."

"Mrs. Madison, Fred works very hard at school. I honestly believe that he is doing his best. I think it would be cruel to present him with harder math when he simply is not ready for it. He is a sweet, conscientious child. He seems content with himself and works hard. He gets confused sometimes, and frustrated—but he usually comes to me when he needs help."

"That is not true," Fred's mother argued. "I work with him every night and I know he is ready for harder material."

"I hope that you will not move Fred in the middle of the year. He has adjusted to this class well. He has many friends and is working hard," the teacher said to her as they walked to the door.

The next day when Fred came to school, he announced to the class and the teacher that he was going to a private school.

Some parents focus *too* much attention on their children. They become overzealous and want desperately to prove that their children are brighter and more advanced than they really are. They tend to overestimate their children's abilities and blame everybody else for their problems. When parents want exceptions made for their children and don't allow them to learn at their own pace, the children often develop an exaggerated sense of their own importance.

Whenever a parent imposes standards on his children that are too high or too unrealistic, the results can be disasterous. Often, parents who push children academically are satisfying their own need to show how smart their children are. A mother may use her child as a status symbol or a father may try to live vicariously through his son. Both are endeavoring to pressure the child to live out their own frustrated ambitions. These parents hold up ill-defined and constantly accelerating goals. The pursuit of these vague goals aimed at perfection can lead to chronic frustration, depression, and despair on the part of the child. He has a difficult time acquiring a good feeling about himself. He is constantly reminded that he "should have tried a little harder" or "done just a little better." Feeling that he always falls short of the goal, he is never pleased with himself. Unless the pattern is changed, he may fulfill his own prophecy and become a failure.

Adults who are perfectionists themselves are often too critical of their children and expect too much too soon. They sometimes find it difficult to praise and tend to take for granted the many small, positive accomplishments of their children. They focus too much on their weaknesses. The child develops feelings of inadequacy and inferiority and feels angry and resentful toward the critical and demanding adult.

We need to help each child feel valued apart from his achievements. We should not confuse high expectations with evidence of love.

Adults should make every effort to examine their own lives and find ways of achieving their own goals so they will not fall into the trap of trying to shape their children into becoming what they would like to have become themselves.

The more fulfilled we are as adults, the fewer unrealistic pressures we will put on our children. Therefore, when we increase our own self-acceptance, we are more free to be accepting of our children, not because of their accomplishments, their looks, or their grades, but just because of their existence.

Homework

> Kevin, 12, was in his room working on a spelling assignment for which he had to know the definitions of several new words. The teacher had written the definitions on a handout, but Kevin had left that at school. Therefore, Kevin's mother made him look up each word in the dictionary so that he could complete the assignment. Kevin did the work under protest, complaining that he was in a hurry to go out to play. He kept calling his mother to come help him decide which definition was the right one. She responded in a very helpful way, at first, but because he called for help so often, her disposition changed. She became irritated with him, scolded and criticized him for being so lazy, and did most of the work herself.

It is doubtful that Kevin profited in any way from his homework. This mother is "getting the education" and Kevin is proving that no one is going to *make* him learn.

Kevin's mother had become his servant—he ordered her around and she obeyed his commands. She did his work for him so he could go out to play.

Homework assignments should be between the teacher and the child. The teacher could provide some sort of reinforcement to go along with homework for students like Kevin who need motivation. Incentives such as tokens, extra free time, time to work on favorite projects or read library books, or freedom to choose partners for a learning game can be given at school for completed homework assignments.

I think it is better for parents to divorce themselves from the homework scene. They *can*, however, play an important role for the child by listening to his complaints, providing him with a good place to study, and demonstrating an interest in books and a curiosity for learning (carrying on stimulating conversations and playing challenging mind games with him, for example, instead of watching T.V.).

I don't think it is especially harmful to make a deal with the child: "For every one-half hour you study before 8:00 p.m., you may earn a point. When you have earned ten points, I will buy you the new tennis shoes you have been wanting." You could work out an arrangement with the teacher that each day Kevin brings his homework assignment in, she will send home a happy face. When Kevin has collected five happy faces, the family will go to his favorite restaurant for supper.

When parents become more involved than this, such as saying, "No T.V. until the homework is done," there is the possibility that children will resort to lying about their assignments. Our goal is for the child to feel the responsibility for his work himself. As long as the parent is willing to assume it for him, he will not become a self-motivated, disciplined, and responsible student.

Parents can help a great deal by talking with their children about homework. "When do you think is the best time for you to do your work? When are you at your best? Do you understand the assignments? Can you do the work? How would you like to set the timer and try to beat the clock with getting your work done? If you finish before the buzzer goes off, you can stay up fifteen minutes later tonight" (or have some other privilege the child enjoys).

Children generally do better in school when parents:

- provide a place for study.
- provide a model for intellectual curiosity (reading, questioning, discussing and problem solving).
- read to the child.
- call out spelling and multiplication tables, when asked.
- talk to and listen to the child.
- show an interest in his work.

- engage the child in kitchen, basement, garage and sports' math. (How many tablespoons do I need for one-half cup of butter? What was the difference in the scores of the two teams?)

- ask the child many questions which he can answer or work to find the solution.

Learning Problems

Children with learning disabilities are just like other children in most ways. They see and hear normally and have average or above average intelligence. They do not look any different, but they do stand out from other children in one way. They do not learn like their peers.

Sometimes these children are overlooked. They just fall further and further behind. Their self concept beings to suffer too, as they see themselves as failures.

Children with learning disabilities exhibit a number of the following traits over a long period of time. (It is important to mention that most children demonstrate some of these difficulties some of the time, but children with learning disabilities exhibit them over and over again.)

- They may have a very short attention span and find it very difficult to complete a task or follow simple directions.

- They may not be able to identify and sort out sounds and show a great deal of confusion when there is a great deal of noise.

- They may mix up numbers, letters and words (937 for 379, god for dog, and aminal for animal).

- Their minds may see one thing while their eyes see another, or they may see them backwards.

- They may have trouble remembering all the parts in a whole. They may forget to put on one shoe.

- They may seem clumsy and uncoordinated. They may often drop and spill things.

- They often confuse directions: left for right, up for down.

- They may be impulsive and fail to consider the consequences of their actions.

- They may not be able to keep their hands to themselves. They want to touch everyone and everybody.

- They may have boundless energy, quickly moving from one activity to another.

- They probably feel that they can't do anything right—that they are different from others—and therefore unlikeable.

Although many professionals label these disorders differently, it is helpful to have a child diagnosed by a team of experts. This can be done in a medical setting or in a mental health, educational, or other facility. It will help to know the specific learning disability or disabilities that characterize your child (perceptual, integrative, memory, motor, sequencing, or language). The diagnosis should result in a definite treatment plan, specifically designed for your child, known as an I.E.P. (individualized educational prescription). You will want to learn ways to help your child at home by building on his strengths rather than magnifying his weaknesses. Some helpful tips for parents of children with learning disabilities are:

- Ask questions. Learn as much as possible about your child's problem.

- Set aside some time each day to be alone with your child. Give him activities to do in which he is guaranteed to succeed.

- Be as patient as possible. Keep directions short and simple.

- Don't allow your child to become overly frustrated. If the task is too difficult, move to something easier. Stop while he is feeling successful.

- Praise the child for even the smallest success. Do not call attention to the mistakes.

- Listen with your eyes and ears. Tune in to him.

- Relax with him. Enjoy your time together.

- Be honest. Don't pretend that there is nothing wrong. He knows better.

- Let him know that help is available. He *can* learn—and you are there to help him.

- Don't blame yourself. Get help when you need it. Talk to other parents with the same problem. Remember that you are human, too, and you have your limitations as well as your own life to live.

The most important role of parents, as I see it, is to "be there"—to listen, reflect feelings, support, care, and show concern—as our children are learning and struggling to assume responsibility for their own lives.

School Problems

For children ages 4 to 8:

Amoss, Berthe. *The Very Worst Thing*. New York: Parent's Magazine Press, 1972. Fiction.

> In this book, a young boy tells the story of his unpleasant experiences as a newcomer in class.

Barkin, Carol and Elizabeth James. *I'd Rather Stay Home*. Milwaukee, Wis.: Raintree Publishers, 1975. Fiction.

> This is a realistic story of a boy overcoming his fear of starting school.

Bradenberg, Franz. *Six New Students*. New York: Greenwillow Books, 1978. Fiction.

> A clever teacher helps a first grader enjoy his first day of school.

Cohen, Miriam. *The New Teacher*. New York: Macmillan Co., 1972. Fiction.

> This is a story of a separation between a group of young children and a much-loved teacher.

Cohen, Miriam. *Will I Have A Friend*? New York: Collier Books, 1967. Fiction.

> This story realistically shows a young boy's anxieties and his initial feeling of loneliness at a new school.

For children ages 8 to 12:

Byars, Betsy Cromer. *The TV Kid*. New York: The Viking Press, 1976. Fiction.

> An exciting story about a young boy's struggle to change his behavior.

Cleary, Beverly. *Ramona The Brave*. New York: William Morrow & Co., 1975. Fiction.

> This amusing story describes a little girl's first year in school.

For children ages 12 to 16:

Blue, Rose. *A Month of Sundays*. New York: Franklin Watts, 1972. Fiction.

> This book tells of the confusion felt by a young boy who is suddenly uprooted and encounters a drastic change in environment.

For adults:

Rogers, Fred and Barry Head. *Mister Rogers Talks With Parents*. New York: Berkley Books, 1983. Nonfiction.

> This book gives clear and practical advice to parents on a wide variety of topics from disabilities to death. One chapter is devoted to early challenges which includes school experiences.

Taking pictures of friends is a good way to keep them "alive" even when you move away.

Chapter Five

Moving

Some individuals adjust to change more easily than others. The basic characteristics we see in babies usually predict behaviors in later life. Some babies cope beautifully when taken to unfamiliar surroundings; others become frantic and uneasy.

For most children adequate preparation makes transitions easier. Many adults fail to realize the importance of including children as they plan a change. They make the mistake of trying to spare them needless worry or anxiety by leaving them out of the decision-making process.

Sometimes parents spring surprises on their children or send them away while important events are taking place in the life of the family. Then they are surprised and mystified when the child responds with bed-wetting, newly acquired fears and nightmares, separation anxiety, aggressiveness, acting out or phobias.

Even young children can sense when change is "in the air." Mothers often report that their babies begin crying an hour before they make preparation to leave them with a sitter.

It is no wonder then, that when a child's familiar world is taken away from him, he usually becomes anxious. If it has happened suddenly or without warning, he begins to fear that it may happen again, anytime, anywhere.

Parents need to be aware of the many ways they can help their child during these important and unsettling times.

> Joanie's family had just moved. Her grandmother, who lived with them, kept four-year-old Joanie during the day while her parents worked.

> Since it was warm and pleasant outdoors, Joanie's grandmother suggested that they go for a walk around the neighborhood, hoping that Joanie could meet some other children and make new friends.

> Joanie cried and refused to leave the house. Her grandmother tried to put her coat on, but Joanie hung on the door frame and protested loudly that she didn't want to go outside. Joanie said that she was afraid her parents were not coming back to this house and she would be left alone to die.

> That night, Joanie didn't want to go to bed. She cried until her parents finally allowed her to sleep with them. Even though she had new furniture which she had helped to select, Joanie was unwilling to sleep alone in her new room.

Easing the Transition

Moving is a difficult transition to make for many adults as well as for most children. Moving disrupts routine, familiarity, and security. It often causes stress, anxiety, and a lowered self concept.

Some suggestions for making it easier:

- Involve the children from the beginning. Discuss the move, its pros and cons. Let them visit the new house before moving into it.

- Give them something concrete to look forward to. For example, two children who have shared a room may be allowed separate bedrooms. It might help to let them pick out the new drapes, rugs, or bedspreads.

- Saying goodbye to friends is always painful. Let the children preserve ties with their old friends as long as they need to through telephone conversations and exchanges of visits. Perhaps if they are enrolled in a school or playgroup in the old community, they may be allowed to finish the current term there. Do not allow them to miss opportunities, however, to meet new friends in the new location.

- Try to keep family schedules constant as much as possible. Find ways to reassure your child that your love will not change, that he will always be as important to you as he is now.

- Be sensitive to the effects of disruption. Realize, for example, how alarming it may be for a three-year-old to come home from nursery school to find her bedroom full of packing boxes. Although it is more convenient to have her out from under foot during actual packing operations, consider letting her stay just long enough to see what is going on. A few days in advance, she may be encouraged to help you pack a few boxes of her special toys.

- Don't hurry to redecorate. It might be better if the child can expect to sleep in the same bed or crib and keep the same stuffed animals and blankets, even if they are worn out and shabby.

- Expect the child to need time to adjust. Be willing to let her regress, keep her light on at night, take a variety of stuffed toys to bed with her.

- Give the child many chances to express her feelings. Talk about her fears, loneliness, memories of her old home. Be willing to sit beside her (rubbing her back, singing), or lie down with her in her bed when she has trouble with the transition. This is probably better than letting the child develop the habit of sleeping with her parents.

Anyone can manage to be miserable in any situation in which she finds herself. On the other hand, it is possible to be reasonably content and happy under even the most trying circumstances. Our children's attitudes will be determined in large part by our reactions to events or surroundings perceived as being "strange." It is up to us to make these experiences adventures, not inconveniences or obstacles.

There are many ways we can help children to adjust to moving to a different culture, as military families are often required to do:

- Try to find out as much as you can about the place you are going, its history, main attractions, climate, and geography. Let the children help you research these facts. Familiarity in this instance helps breed security.

- If the assignment involves another language or a regional dialect of English that may be unfamiliar, any background in that language is helpful. Even if only a few words are learned, at least they will afford an element of recognition and understanding.

- Let the children know what to expect, both good and bad. If partings from pets, for example, will be required, tell the children rather than having the animal simply disappear one morning. Let them help find it a home and meet the people who will care for it.

- Allow the child the dignity of his grief at parting from the pets and from friends. It does not help to say, "Oh, you'll forget Roger in two weeks." It is acceptable to talk about what kinds of new friends he may encounter or about how he first met his current buddy after initial loneliness, but don't deny him his grief.

- Be wary of plunging children into situations for which they are not ready. Many of us assume that children will adjust easily and quickly to new surroundings simply because they are children. Some people feel that by placing a child in an environment where only a strange language is used, the child will "pick up" that language quickly and fluently. Some will. Others, however, will become bewildered and overcome by such an experience. Be aware of your own child's needs and nature and encourage him to adapt in whichever way is most natural and helpful to him.

- On the other hand, do not allow him or yourself to just sit, pretending you never left your former home. You will be denying yourselves a richness of experience that cannot be attained in any other way.

- Adopt some local customs or holiday traditions to your own use. Learn to cook and enjoy ethnic foods particular to your area. Acquire household furnishings or memorabilia from the various areas in which you have lived, and let the children share the stories of their background and purpose.

- Among your "carry-ons" or express shipment, include familiar belongings and perhaps a scrapbook or pictures of the old home surroundings to remind your child of how things were and will be again.

Talk with the child as much as possible about the move, even if you think he's too young to understand. Young children need to hear things over and over before they begin to conceptualize what is really happening and realize how it may affect them.

Military Deployments

The dreaded day had arrived. For several months, the family had been talking about Bob's deployment—making plans, taking care of last minute details, checking on repairs and appliances, the car, the house.

The bags were packed and good-byes had been said. Everyone had cried.

"Time to go," Bob called to Merissa, 8, and Brian, 4.

No answer.

"Hurry up. Where did you go?"

"Maria, where are the children?" he called impatiently.

"I don't know. Children, come on."

"Mom, come here," Merissa called from upstairs.

Quickly, Maria ran up to see what was keeping the children.

"Look what happened. Brian was flushing the toilet, and it over-flowed." The bathroom floor was covered with water.

Brian was crying. "Don't tell Daddy. He'll be mad." Without success he was trying to wipe up the floor. He was getting his new clothes all wet.

"Oh, Brian, how could you? Here, move. Go change your clothes. Hurry. We'll be late."

"Maria, what's going on up there? Hurry." Bob called.

"We're coming. Just a minute."

By the time Brian's clothes were changed and the bathroom cleaned up, they were about 15 minutes late leaving.

All the way to the ship, Bob was quiet. Worried, Mother tried to reassure him. "I'm sure we'll make it on time."

"I don't know. We are cutting it short. Thanks to you kids, I might be late. Do you realize what that would mean—if I was late?"

Merissa and Brian sat quietly in the back seat, scared to say a word.

It's not unusual when there are impending separations for tempers to flare and unexpected mishaps to occur. Separations from loved ones are difficult and if there is something unpleasant to focus on and to get mad at, leaving loved ones becomes more bearable.

Many members of military families confess that the few days and hours before a deployment are often filled with arguing, fighting, and disagreements. When the ship pulls out, they feel devastated to realize that their last hours together, instead of being tender and sweet, were full of discord.

Jimmy, nine, had always made good grades in school. Frances had never worried about her son's school performance.

One day his teacher called and told Frances that Jimmy was falling down in his school work. He had forgotten to bring his homework, and he had trouble keeping his mind on his studies. She asked for a conference.

Frances made an appointment and went to see Jimmy's teacher.

"Mrs. Blake, I can't imagine what has happened to Jimmy. Up until Christmas he was a model student—never gave me a minute's worry. But after Christmas he started going downhill. Do you know what could have happened to him?"

Frances nodded sadly, "I guess it's his father being gone. You know his ship went out the day after Christmas. I knew Jimmy missed his dad, but I guess I never realized how much."

Parents need to be aware of the problems which often occur when families are separated. Young children frequently think their father chose to go away. They blame themselves and believe that it is because of their naughtiness. Fearing that their mother might leave too if they misbehave again, they wonder who would take care of them. What would they do?

The fears and uncertainties cause the child to be hostile, angry, defiant, and sad. His feelings may be expressed in tearful moodiness, withdrawal, or physical complaints. He may shrink from attending school and extracurricular activities.

A son might develop an obsessive need to be with mother, to be like her, or to take over for the absent father. If she starts relying on him to make decisions and meet her emotional needs, he could become confused about his place in the family.

Some of the ways that families can help to cope with these frequent separations are:

- Admit feelings of sadness, self-doubt and fear, dread and loneliness. The "stiff upper lip" approach often misleads

Childhood
Stress

children into thinking that their feelings are unacceptable or bad. Encourage honest dialogue.

- Try to keep father and children real to each other. Send photographs and tapes of dinner conversations, bedtime prayers, and arguments over the "biggest piece of cake." Before he leaves, the father might tape some of the children's favorite stories and songs, so that they can listen to his voice anytime they want to. Fathers can also send home recordings of the ship's churning engines, the clanking machinery, and the cries of the sea birds.

- Measure the passage of time in concrete ways—on calendars, by marking maps, or tearing links off a paper chain for every day or week he is away.

- Keep the father informed—about the bad things that happen, not just the good. Don't worry about "sparing" him. He needs to be in on the family interests. Don't save surprises for his return.

- Stay busy and involved in activities with other adults and families. Find support groups. Make new friends.

Jeff had just returned from a six-month cruise in the Mediterranean. His family had looked forward to this day for months. Donna, four, and Danny, six, had stayed up late the night before, decorating the house for the big occasion. They had gotten up early to greet the ship.

Finally, the family was reunited and eating their first meal together. Jeff noticed that Danny was eating meat with his fingers. "Hey, son, what do you think forks are for? What's happened to your manners?"

"The meat's too chewy and I can't cut it with my fork," Danny explained as he continued eating with his fingers.

"Danny, do what your father said. Use your fork," Janet said. Danny acted as if he hadn't heard.

"Son, did you hear your mother? Now, look here, young man. I don't know what you have been getting away with while I was gone, but you are going to straighten up, I can tell you that. I didn't come home to a bunch of uncivilized pigs. Now you either eat with your fork or leave the table. Do you understand?"

Danny started crying and left the table. He ran upstairs and slammed the door to his room.

Janet started crying. "Why did you have to get on him the first night you were home? He has bragged to everyone about his father coming home, and now look what you've done. A happy homecoming this has turned out to be." She started clearing away the plates.

While fathers are away, mothers must cope—with the house, lawn, budget, cars, misbehaving children, and loneliness. Being outnumbered, sometimes four to one, they adopt more cooperative and democratic parenting styles. Children are given more freedom and responsibility, adjustments are made, and a routine is established in which everyone can function reasonably well.

And then the father comes home. Another adjustment. After months of cherished memories centered around the picture on his desk—children under the Christmas tree smiling into the camera—he is unprepared for the food fights, bloody noses, wet beds, and bathroom language.

Having spent every waking hour giving orders and having them obeyed, receiving orders and "hopping to" himself, he is obviously shaken when his two-year-old will have nothing to do with him, his six-year-old refuses to obey his first instructions, and his nine-year-old walks out of the room in the middle of a conversation. His image of the family is shattered, and his own self image cracks a little too.

The mother is uneasy because she is afraid that she will be blamed for letting things fall apart. She can predict the children's reaction when father tries to whip them back into line with his authoritarian methods. She feels torn—trying to give back some of the authority and meeting resistance from the children. Her needs have changed too. Readjusting to a man she hasn't seen in six months is not easy.

Re-entry is difficult for all families, but military families seem to have more than their share of changes. Some suggestions to help with re-entry are:

- While the father is gone, don't fall into the trap of using "just wait until your father comes home" as the ultimate threat. This makes it difficult for children to look forward to his return.

- Give children time and space to adapt to both the separations and returns. Take your cues from the child. It takes time to shift gears and to warm up.

- Don't expect too much too soon. Each relationship needs to be cultivated, cherished, and handled carefully. Since the husband-wife team is the "hub of the wheel," it might be wise for them to take a few days to become reacquainted without the complication of children.

- Then allow time for the children to warm up gradually—ideally one-on-one as time and circumstances permit.

- Discuss issues openly—what Dad will do now that he is back and who is in charge of what.

- Know that things will never be the same as they were before. Children grow and change. Adults change too. With luck, understanding, flexibility, and careful planning, you can fall in love again each time you are reunited and find something just as strong and good and solid as families who have never been separated.

Military families need to depend on each other. If they are sensitive to the problems they face and learn to develop the skills necessary for coping, they will share many unique experiences that can enrich their lives and draw them closer.

Whatever the circumstances, separations from loved ones are difficult, but, when families are aware of potential problems they can anticipate and prevent crises.

The mental health of the adults involved is the single most important factor which will determine the effect of the separation on the children.

For example, while her husband is gone, the mother needs to be careful to look out for her own needs. It is easy for conscientious mothers to fall into a routine where they devote all their time to their children and taking care of their children's needs. It is important for mothers to feel that their own lives are fulfilled.

This can be done in many ways—talking with other wives in the same situation, joining wives' clubs, going to a movie, getting involved in regular physical exercise, taking classes in a local university, or learning a new hobby. It might be helpful for her to consider a paying job to keep her life in better perspective. Some jobs can be done at home, such as typing, keeping children, or teaching piano.

It is often helpful if several mothers go together to organize a babysitting co-op where they take turns caring for children and getting breaks away.

In the long run, each parent must realize that she alone is responsible for her own happiness. If she has developed successful coping techniques, her children will learn these important coping devices from her. If she is truly proud to be a part of military life, her children will grow up to feel the same way.

When children leave their friends, familiar surroundings, and loved ones, it is important to realize the difficulties involved. Some further suggestions for making it more bearable are:

- Give the child as much accurate information as he can handle. Talk about the move, the changes, the unpleasant parts as well as the advantages.

- Let the child have input. Allow him to make some decisions concerning what he takes with him and what he leaves behind.

- Make the transition as easy as possible by allowing the child to keep with him favored and special belongings.

- Give him an opportunity to express his sadness and fears. Be sure that he is given time to say "good-bye."

- Acquaint him with information about the place where he is going. If it is not possible for him to see it first-hand, provide pictures and let him talk with others who have been there.

- Expect protest, anxiety, ambivalence, aggression, and anger. Some of these emotions help to make the separations more bearable.

- Don't burn the bridges. Keep lines of communication open with the people from the past and let the ties become severed gradually and naturally.

When adults make transitions easily and honestly, the children are likely to follow their example.

Moving

For children ages 4 to 8:

Duczman, Linda. *The Baby-Sitter*. Milwaukee WI: Raintree Publishers, 1977, Nonfiction.

    A photo essay describing a young child's fears about having a baby-sitter for the first time.

Fisher, Aileen Lucia. *My Mother and I*. New York: Thomas Y. Crowell Co., 1967. Fiction.

    A young girl's loneliness after her sudden separation from her mother is keenly felt, as is her happiness when they are reunited.

Hickman, Martha Whitmore. *My Friend William Moved Away*. Nashville, Tenn.: Abingdon Press, 1979. Fiction.

    This first person account emphasizes the loneliness that a young boy feels after his close friend moves.

Hoffman, Mary Ann and Filomena Sitler. *A Special Family*. Color illustrations by Susan Strok. Annapolis, Md: Naval Institute Press, 1981. Fiction.

    This story focuses on a Navy Father's deployment and how it affects his family.

Mack, Nancy. *I'm Not Going*. Milwaukee, WI: Raintree Publishers, 1976. Fiction.

> A very believable story that focuses on a young child's negative reaction to moving.

Tobias, Tobi. *Moving Day*. New York: Alfred A. Knopf, 1976. Fiction.

> This story describes a family move from the child's perspective.

Waber, Bernard. *Ira Sleeps Over*. Boston: Houghton Mifflin Co., 1972. Fiction.

> This is a humorous story about a boy who sleeps over at a friend's house.

For children ages 8 to 12:

Banks, Ann and Nancy Evans. *Goodbye, House—A Kid's Guide to Moving*. New York: Harmony Books, 1980. Nonfiction.

> This book describes a child's diary of a move in scrapbook form.

Stolz, Mary Slattery. *A Wonderful, Terrible Time*. New York: Harper and Row Publishers, Inc., 1967. Fiction.

> This book describes two girls and their different experiences at a summer camp.

For adults:

Friedrich, Barbara and Sally Hulstrand. *Did Somebody Pack the Baby?* Englewood Cliffs, NJ: Prentice-Hall, 1978. Nonfiction.

> A guidebook for moving which includes chapters on moving overseas and moving with children.

Hoffman, Mary Ann and Filomena Sitler. *The Parent's Guide to Navy Life*. Annapolis: The Naval Institute Press, 1981. Nonfiction.

> This book explains how the Navy is organized; provides information on finances, privileges, and benefits; and gives advice on how to handle moves, deployments, and the Navy lifestyle. An excellent bibliography on military life is included.

Childhood
Stress

Many parents of teenagers have a hard time realizing their children are growing up and have minds, needs, wishes, and lives of their own. As parents, we have to convince ourselves that our teenagers want the freedom to make their own decisions and learn to be in control of their lives.

Chapter Six

Independence and Letting Go

The job of the parent is to work himself "out of a job." Our goal is to provide our children with a "tool kit" that contains all the skills necessary for a productive and challenging life.

We only have a few years—about sixteen, I'd say—to do the job.

We must start early, when the child is very young, to get him started on the road to independence. We have to allow and prepare him to gradually become his own boss, to make good decisions on his own behalf, and to assume eventually the responsibility for his own life.

In the process, the parent has to be careful not to make the child *too* important. The parent cannot afford to meet his needs through the child, for each will become *too* dependent on the other, creating an unhealthy symbiotic relationship. When the time comes for the normal separations to occur, it will be extremely difficult, if not impossible, for each to let go of the other.

Therefore it is necessary for parents to know early on what their job is all about so that they can effectively and successfully raise their child— to let him go. Then, he will feel free to return willingly and happily— to take his place as a caring and compassionate adult—able to relate interdependently in a mature and mutually satisfying way.

Separation Anxiety

Excited about the trip to the airport, Amy, was walking toward the gate with her mother and grandparents. Upon reaching the customs desk, she was told that she couldn't go any further.

Since she had expected to walk with her mother all the way to the plane, Amy became upset and began to cry. Violently pulling away from her mother and grandparents, she went to stand by the wall. All three adults approached her, but she wouldn't be quieted.

Yanking her to a seat in the corridor, her mom began to scold. "How can I love you if you act like that? How can you act this way in front of your grandparents? You will hurt their feelings. You have ruined my last day with you. I don't think I want to come back and see you any more."

Amy proceeded to cry harder and harder.

Her mother left with Amy still crying.

Amy didn't understand why she couldn't go with her mother. Their last time together ended in sadness and frustration, leaving Amy with the fear that perhaps her mother wouldn't return. The grandparents were left with a forlorn child.

Separations are hard, and a sudden shift in plans makes them even harder. Often children have mistaken notions and such disappointments are inevitable. However, adults need to be sensitive to what is going on within and try to help the child over the necessary hurdles.

In this case, Amy's mother was trying to make her behave appropriately by shaming her. Such techniques usually backfire and cause additional problems.

Ideally, time should have been spent with Amy ahead of time preparing her for the separation. She might have been encouraged to help her mother pack or look for pictures in magazines showing airplanes or places where she might be going. She could select some postcards which her mother would send at the first stop or destination.

Of course, it would have been better if Amy understood airport procedures. They might have role played the parting scene and Amy could have been told why the airport has rules and regulations which protect the passengers and workers.

At least her mother could have sat down with Amy, when she realized her disappointment, and told her how sad she was to be leaving her. She could have given her something special to keep as a reminder of their time together (a compact or lipstick tube) or told her something she could look forward to (a trip to the park with her grandparents or a phone call from her mother that night).

When it was discovered that Amy's expectations could not be realized, an alternate suggestion could have been quickly made. "Let's find a window where you can watch my plane while it takes off."

Leaving loved ones is difficult for most of us. Children need extra help, for they lack our perspective and often feel devastated when someone they need and depend on is going away.

Starting School

Mike and Marc, 6-year-old twins, were excited about going to first grade. Their mother had taken them to visit the school, to meet the teacher, and to meet some of the other children who were going to be in their classes.

Rachel had agreed reluctantly to separating the twins into separate classrooms. They had always been together in preschool, Sunday School, and at home, where they slept in the same room. The teachers and the principal stood firm, though, in feeling that it would be best for the children to be separated.

The boys were anxious to ride the school bus the first day, but Rachel wanted to take them to make sure everything went well. Instead of dropping them off, she went into the school with them. First she went with Mike to his class and got him settled. Then she took Marc to his room. He had always been the more dependent twin, and she was anxious about how he would adjust to being without his brother. She sensed that he was nervous.

Rachel decided to stay at school all day. She remained in Marc's room most of the time, reassuring him frequently that she was still there. Occasionally, she would make short visits to Mike's room to check on him.

At the end of the day, Rachel went to the principal's office. She had decided that Marc couldn't handle being away from his brother, and she requested that they both be put in the same classroom.

The principal said that he would talk with the teachers about it.

This mother is overly involved in her children's lives. She needs to remove herself and let the boys learn to fend for themselves. As long as she stays nearby, they will sense her uneasiness and will probably feel apprehensive too. By behaving in this way, she is silently conveying to them the message, "You are not ready to make it on your own. You still need me."

It would be healthier for them all if she made an effort to convey the opposite message, "You are ready now to take care of yourself. You are old enough and mature enough, and I trust your ability to handle yourselves in this new situation."

Unconsciously, Rachel may need her boys to stay dependent on her. If this is so, she would be wise to develop some outside interests or get a part-time job to help wean herself away.

Teenagers—Growing Away

Marianne, 12, didn't want to go to school. She told her mother that she felt sick. "Why don't you let me stay home with you? What are you going to do today?" Marianne asked her mother.

"Nothing, honey. Just think, I don't have anything to do today, and you can go to school. That's more fun than I'll be having. Just staying home and cleaning the house and missing you. I'll be right here when you get home—waiting for you."

"But I want to stay with you. Please, Mom. My stomach hurts. Just like it did last week. You remember when I threw up and had to stay home? I feel like I'm going to be sick again."

"Now, Marianne, I think you're all right. I took you to the doctor and he couldn't find anything wrong with you. Why don't you want to go to school? Don't you like school? Your teacher seems nice. She says you're doing fine in school, you've been bringing home good papers. Last week you got two A's. I can't figure out what's wrong. C'mon. you'll be fine. Jenny will be expecting you to meet her at the bus."

Marianne listened in silence. When her mother finished she left the room.

Her mother heard her in the bathroom, throwing up.

Marianne stayed home from school.

Marianne has a form of school phobia. Conscientiously, her mother has checked out the causes—possibly physical and possibly the school environment. Neither of these seems to be the problem.

Marianne really wants to stay home with her mother to "take care of her." Without meaning to, her mother has made Marianne feel *too* important in her life. Because she has not turned Marianne "loose," the child finds it difficult to become absorbed in her own life—in school, in her friends, and in her own needs.

Marianne's mother has done what many well-meaning and conscientious parents do: in order to make the child feel important and to build her self–concept, she has given the impression that she is her mother's spark plug and that until she returns home again, her mother will be lonely and sad.

In other words, for the "right" reasons, the mother has done the "wrong" thing. Consequently, mother and child are "stuck" together and need to become "unstuck."

Instead of trying to convince Marianne that she has "nothing to do" but wait for her daughter to come home, her mother would be wise to get herself involved in activities she enjoys—take an exercise, crocheting, or cake decorating class, a course in computers, typing or Spanish, do volunteer work, or get a part-time job. That way, Marianne would be free of the responsibility of keeping her mother happy and being the center of her life.

Then, when Marianne suggests staying home, her mother can truthfully tell her daughter that she will be busy—going to her job or class—while at the same time reassuring her that she will be back before Marianne gets home from school (or has made provision for adequate supervision).

When Marianne's mother is enthusiastic about her own life, mentioning her new interests and excitement about what she is learning, she will begin to loosen her ties to Marianne, thus allowing the child to do the same. Then, Marianne will be able to put her energies into her own life, becoming involved in twelve-year-old interests and activities.

Although the child may initially protest (most of us resist growth and change), and the transition may be difficult, the long-term result will be well worth the effort. Both will enjoy and appreciate each other *more* when neither feels responsible for the other's happiness.

Many parents of teenagers have a hard time realizing their children are growing up and have minds, needs, wishes, and lives of their own. Just as a baby wants to talk and a toddler wants to walk, a teenager wants the freedom to make his own decisions and learn to be in control of his own life.

As parents, we have to convince ourselves that our children have to learn on their own. They will make mistakes and do things the hard way, but that is the essence of growth. We can no longer protect them from the winds, shelter them from the storms, or shield them from the dangers of life. We must let them go without us into world unfamiliar and unknown to us.

Teenagers have a strong need to be independent. Unfortunately, parents need to be needed, and that stands in the way of willingly letting them go. We would like to hold on. Letting go requires strength, generosity and love.

The penalty for trying to hold on too long is resentment, bitterness, rebellion, and deceit. But the child who is given the freedom to travel on his own rocky road will return one day with gratitude and respect, ready to establish a lifetime friendship with the parents who were wise enough to let him go.

> Carol, 17, came hurrying into the room where her mother was watching TV.
>
> "Oh, I didn't hear you come in. I'm glad you're home. I've missed you so much today," Pearle said as she got up and turned off the TV.
>
> "What's wrong, Mother? You look sad," Carol gave her mother a hug.
>
> "I don't know, honey, it's just been one of those days. I really don't feel very well."
>
> "I'm sorry, Mom. Oh, is it all right with you if I go to the movies with Jennifer? We thought maybe we would go early enough to pick up some supper before the show. Is that okay?"
>
> Pearle looked disappointed. "Well, if that's what you want. I had thought maybe we could go shopping. I really don't want to stay home with your father tonight. He's been yelling at me again and I wanted to get out. But that's all right. I don't want to interrupt your plans. You go ahead. I'll stay home."
>
> "Oh, gee, Mom, I'm sorry. You and Dad had another argument? About my staying out late last night? Oh, gee, Mom. It was, wasn't it? You didn't want to let me know. But I can tell. I'm sorry."

Pearle didn't respond—just sadly shook her head.

"I tell you what, Mother. Why don't I call Jennifer and tell her that I'll go with her some other night? Why don't we go shopping, like you said? I think that would be fun."

Carol's mother perked up. "Are you sure? Are you sure you don't mind? I don't want to upset your plans."

Carol called Jennifer and canceled their plans. When she came back to the den, Pearle had become quite animated. "Maybe we can look for a new dress for you. But don't tell your father. He would be mad. And I don't need that."

Pearle is trying to meet her emotional needs through her daughter. This is dangerous, because it could result in an enmeshed relationship between Carol and her mother—where the girl feels too responsible for her mother's happiness and well-being. When a child is "too connected" to a parent, she finds it difficult, if not impossible, to make the necessary separation that is a normal developmental need.

Carol should develop close relationships with people her own age, and she cannot do this if Pearle continues to make her feel guilty.

Pearle is also trying to escape the problems in her marriage relationship by confiding in Carol and not confronting the issue head-on with her husband, a dangerous pattern for families to adopt.

Leaving Home

Jeannette and Steve, 18, planned to do some last-minute shopping for items he needed for college. They had agreed to leave home at 9 a.m.

Realizing that Steve was still asleep at 8:30, Jeanette went into his room.

"Hey, Son, don't you need to get up? It's 8:30, and we wanted to leave at 9."

No answer.

"Steve are you awake?" She reached over and tapped his arm.

"Leave me alone. I'm getting up. Get off my case," Steve snapped at his mother.

"I was just trying to be helpful. That's some way to treat me when I've set aside the day to go shopping with you! If that's the way you are going to talk to me, you can just forget it. I don't care whether we go or not. These things are for you, not me." Mother left the room.

In a few minutes, Mother heard Steve in the shower.

She got ready for their shopping trip and waited for him to come downstairs.

"I'm hungry," Steve announced loudly as he came down the stairs, tucking in his shirttail.

"You don't have time for breakfast if we are going to do all the shopping we need this morning. It's 9:30 already and we had planned to leave at 9. Maybe we can pick up something to eat at the mall."

"My gosh, Mom, you're always hassling me. You have to have everything your way, don't you? I'm sick and tired of having to listen to you. I'll be glad to get away from here."

"Well, that's a fine way to talk to me. Just forget the shopping. I'm not going anywhere with you. You don't deserve anything new. I have more important things to do this morning."

Jeanette picked up her car keys and left. All day she felt resentful, confused, and cheated. She had looked forward to her day with Steve and felt like crying everytime she thought about it. At noon, she called home to try to make amends, but there was no answer.

Separations are hard. In fact, they are so difficult for many of us that the only way we can stand the pain is to create a distance between us and the ones from whom we are going to be separate.

It is easier to leave someone we are mad at than someone we love and need. Therefore, as a safety device, we often find reasons to be angry. We fuss or become obnoxious in order to be sure that the other person will return the anger. Otherwise, the separation might truly be unbearable.

Impending separations are often accompanied by tension. Since Steve was leaving home for the first time, it might be that expressing anger at his mother helped him to deal with the real hurts and anxieties that were lying just beneath the surface.

It is a good idea to talk about such feelings when a separation is inevitable. Parting is easier to deal with when the underlying emotions are faced and don't have to be camouflaged by trumped-up reasons to explode.

The following was written the night we took our third and last child away to college:

> Everywhere I looked, I saw mothers, fathers and co-eds carrying boxes, stereos, suitcases, garment bags, shelves.
>
> Some were embracing for the last time. Looks of embarrassment, nervously glancing around, from a few. Some said their good-byes quickly, others held on tightly. Some wept openly. It was almost too painful to watch.
>
> The weather was more like summer than fall. The air was full of emotion. The parents looked tired and spent. Their children looked excited and energetic.
>
> The trip up had been pleasant—some small talk, some serious. Mostly silence. There was nothing to say that hadn't been said.
>
> We had seen many other cars loaded down, U-Hauls, stationwagons with bikes and beds strapped to back or top. I had wondered if they were talking, giving last-minute advice, or had they, too, been quietly lost in their own thoughts?

It was almost time: my turn to say good-bye to our youngest, our last child to leave home.

One more embrace. One last, "When will you call? I love you." No more words. Only tears.

As we drove off, his silhouette became a blur through my misty eyes. Then we turned the corner, and he was gone.

There was nothing to say. Only my private thoughts. For miles we drove in silence. Words could not take away the hurt—the lump in my throat. I let myself cry.

I never dreamed the years would go so fast. It seemed only a little while ago that we were bringing him home from the hospital.

Could it possibly be over? Is he ready? Did we give enough? Did we give too much?

I will miss him so much—his laughter, his playfulness. He helped me to recapture my own childlikeness.

What paradoxes life has to offer: pride—he's grown up; pain—he's leaving; pleasure—he brought to us; suffering—we will miss him.

There would be a void to fill.

Looking back there were many times of joy, but there were other times too, times of worry, pain, frustration, uncertainty, anger, hurt.

I didn't want to think about that now, but, somehow deep inside, I knew it was true.

There had been days when my patience was thin, my energy gone, my strength sapped, and still more was needed. There were days when I couldn't decide—should I insist? ignore? allow? say yes? or no? set limits? deny? give?

Being a parent is not easy, nor without worry and frustration.

It brings with it pain as well as pleasure; tears as well as laughter.

The paradoxes of life!

How would it feel to get home to a house that was too quiet and straight and clean? I wasn't anxious to find out. I was in no hurry. We took our time.

There would be fewer groceries to buy, smaller meals to cook, less laundry, fewer conflicts, less worry. I would have more time to call my own—to read, write, rest, visit, travel, relax.

Life goes on.

There is work to do—new tasks to accomplish, new mountains to climb.

I am about to burst with mixed emotions: happiness/sadness; excitement/fear; eagerness/dread.

Will this lump in my throat ever go away?

Separation

For children ages 4 to 8:

Adams, Florence. *Mushy Eggs*. New York: G. P. Putnam's Sons, 1973. Fiction.

> This book relates a young boy's feelings about his working mother, his absent father, and his kind babysitter.

For children ages 8 to 12:

Greenfield, Eloise. *Talk About a Family*. New York: J. B. Lippincott Co., 1978. Fiction.

> A young girl is angry and confused, because her parents cannot work out their differences and keep the family together.

Mann, Peggy. *My Dad Lives in a Downtown Hotel*. New York: Doubleday & Co., Inc., 1973. Fiction.

> This book is a compendium of feelings a boy would have after his parents separate and the anguish felt by parents in this situation.

Rogers, Helen Spelman. *Morris and His Brave Lion*. New York: McGraw-Hill Book Co., 1975. Fiction.

> This book conveys a little boy's emotions as he tries to understand the change in family relationships.

For children ages 12 to 16:

Arundel, Honor. *A Family Failing*. Nashville, TN: Thomas Nelson, Inc., 1972. Fiction.

> This first-person narrative realistically portrays the disintegration of a marriage and a family.

Bach, Alice. *A Father Every Few Years*. New York: Harper & Row Publishers, Inc., 1977. Fiction.

> This is a story of a boy who desperately wants a father for himself and a husband for his mother.

For adults:

Ramos, Suzanne. *Teaching Your Child to Cope with Crisis*. New York: David McKay Co., 1975. Nonfiction.

> This book offers advice on how parents can help their children deal with certain events, including parental separations.

Rowlands, Peter. *Children Apart*. New York: Pantheon Books, 1973. Nonfiction.

> This book outlines many suggestions for handling children's separations from their parents.

Childhood
Stress

Sometimes withdrawn, ill-tempered, and confused, the young adolescent needs support and understanding from the adults who care.

Chapter Seven

Depression

It is estimated that approximately 400,000 American children suffer from what is now recognized as childhood depression. This is not a temporary case of the blues but rather a pervasive sadness which paralyzes a child and keeps him from entering into the usual tasks of childhood.

Although depression can have many causes, frequently it is triggered by some kind of loss, such as that of a parent through divorce, death, or sudden illness.

Child therapists tell us that children as young as four can be deeply unhappy and even self-destructive. Preschoolers have been known to strangle themselves, jump out of buildings, or set fire to themselves. In 1976, there were five reported cases of children, ages five to nine, who succeeded in killing themselves; and in 1979, there were 151 reported suicides of children ages ten to fourteen. During that same year, there were 1,788 suicides among children fifteen to nineteen.

These are the reported cases! The chances are great that many reported accidents are actually suicides, covered up to look like accidents.

Moodiness

When the phone rang, it was for nine-year-old Tommy. When Sandra called him, she found her son asleep across his bed. She tried to shake him awake. "Tommy, Brent is on the phone. He wants to come over to play. Tommy, wake up. Brent is on the phone."

"I don't want to play," Tommy muttered, as he turned over to go back to sleep.

Sandra explained to Brent that Tommy was asleep and she couldn't get him to wake up. She was sorry. When he woke up, she would get him to call.

Tommy's mother was worried. She and his father had noticed a lot of differences lately.

His personality had changed from that of a happy-go-lucky, out-going, lovable little boy to that of a sad, bored, and lazy child. Instead of going out to play after school, he spent more and more time sleeping in the afternoons. When he wasn't asleep, he was watching T.V., but rarely seemed to laugh or enjoy what he was watching.

Although he used to hurry to the school bus, recently Tommy had balked and sometimes refused to go to school. After talking with the teacher, Sandra discovered that he exhibited the same characteristics in class too. The teacher said that she has to remind him constantly to pay attention, get busy, or follow through on the instructions.

The teacher suggested that Tommy see a child psychiatrist.

The doctor confirmed the fact that Tommy was suffering from childhood depression.

Experts tell us that one in twenty-five children from the ages of seven to twelve suffers from some form of depression; half of these children exhibit suicidal tendencies.

It is encouraging to know that childhood depression is curable and that the sooner it is detected, the better the chances are for full recovery.

Signs of childhood depression are:

- Persistent unhappiness which pervades every aspect of the child's life.

- Constant "putting oneself down": "No one likes me. I am fat and ugly."

- Exaggerated guilt over minor misbehavior or happenings, "I know it is my fault that Daddy got sick."

- Increased irritability and boredom even though circumstances have not changed and the same friends and activities are still available.

- Changes in sleeping and eating patterns: can't sleep or eat, or sleep or eat too much.

- New physical ailments: headaches, chest pains, stomachaches.

- School phobia: doesn't want to go to school, can't concentrate.

- Constant talking about death: parent's, pet's, or own.

A child who shows one or more of the symptoms mentioned above is in need of help. There is excellent professional help available.

There are precautions parents can take to prevent depression.

- Give your child many successes. Help him to develop skills and mastery so that he will feel good about himself and his accomplishments. A child who is capable and who can do many things well will have a good self esteem.

- Help your child to become independent. If he knows he can take care of his own needs, the child stays busy and enjoys the feeling of competence.

- Be sure that his school life is working well for him. Do not subject him to repeated failures and defeat.

- Watch for sudden changes in his personality.

- Be open-minded to the fact that your child is suffering and needs help. Don't blame and berate yourself. Look for help.

- Don't push your child *out* when there is family tragedy or change. Let him see you "feel" what it is that you feel: sadness, loneliness, disappointment, anger, grief.

- Let your child know that you are concerned if he seems down. Talk with him gently, laying the groundwork for him to express his feelings. Don't ever minimize his feelings since they are very real to him.

- If you are emotionally unable to deal with your child, get someone else to do it. Often an older sibling can help.

- Don't stop loving him, but don't overindulge him. Enforce the usual discipline and be consistent.

- If you are having emotional problems yourself, seek professional help.

Another informal and excellent way in which parents can help their children to "open up" and talk about what they are feeling is to encourage all family members to play a "complete the sentence" game. This can be done around the dinner table, riding in the car, or any other time when there is an opportunity for discussion and sharing. Some suggestions, for starters, are:

I would like to ....

I am happy when ....

I am scared when ....

It makes me mad when ....

I wish that my mother would ....

I wish that my father would ....

I wish that my mother would not ....

I wish that my father would not ....

I wish that my teacher would ....

I wish that my teacher would not ....

I don't like it when my mother ....

I don't like it when my father ....

I don't like it when my teacher ....

I don't think it's fair that ....

I wish that I could ....

I wish that I didn't have to ....

I am afraid that ....

I am glad that ....

I'll be glad when ....

When I'm a parent, I will ....

When I'm a parent, I will not ....

It is important to allow and encourage the child to say whatever is on his mind, without having the adult or anyone else become defensive or try in any way to "talk him out" of his feelings.

This game has become a favorite in many families, and children ask to play it over and over. It has opened the door for many enlightening and thought-provoking discussions. It can often uncover the root of the child's depression.

Suicidal Tendencies

The experts are alarmed at the increasing rate of suicide, especially among adolescents. The estimates are still low, because an unknown number of deaths reported as accidents may actually be suicides.

The statistics indicate that youngsters who succeed at suicide are generally brighter and taller than average. Many are known to have had antisocial or depressive personalities and one-half have either been receiving psychiatric assistance or recognized as being in need of such help.

Many of them had skipped school the previous day in order to plan carefully the place, circumstances, and time of death. The ones who left notes stated a fear of school or personal failure or loss.

In early adolescence, suicidal tendencies may be characterized by anger and disorganized or erratic behavior. By late adolescence, the tendencies may be seen in disillusionment, dissatisfaction, and a sense of loss.

In one study (Golombek and Garfinkel 1983) of 1500 successful suicides and 500 unsuccessful, it was found that the better students made the most serious attempts. Only ten percent of those who were successful were out of work or school, while fifty-three percent of the attempters had either dropped out of school or were below grade level.

Some startling statistics about teen suicide are:

- The suicide rate for young people is increasing ten times faster than that for any other age group.
- Four out of every five people who kill themselves have attempted suicide previously.
- Nine out of ten teen suicide attempts take place in the home.
- Seven out of ten teen suicide attempts occur while one or both parents are at home.
- Seventy-one percent of young people attempting suicide come from divorced homes.
- Less than one and one-third percent of attempted suicides are successful. (These are National Institute of Mental Health and National Center for Health statistics.)

The following resources are available:

Hotlines

Two international suicide-prevention organizations have centers in the United States that operate twenty-four-hour hotlines.

CONTACT has 104 centers in the U.S. To obtain a list of

CONTACT centers and their hotline numbers, write: CONTACT USA, 900 S. Arlington Ave., Harrisburg, PA 17109.

The Samaritans have 215 centers worldwide, although only seven are located in the U.S., in Chicago, New York City, Lawrence, Falmouth, and Boston, Massachusetts, Providence, Rhode Island, and Washington, D.C.

To find the center closest to you, call the American Association of Suicidology during business hours at (303) 692-0985 or write the organization for an annually updated directory of centers: 2459 S. Ash, Denver, CO 80222.

Treatment

To locate long-term therapeutic treatment, usually offered by community mental health clinics, contact either the National Mental Health Association, (1800 N. Kent St., Arlington, VA 22209 at (703) 528-6405) or the National Institute of Mental Health (Public Inquiries, 5600 Fishers Ln., Rockville, MD 20857 at (301) 443-4515).

For Adults:

Durkheim, Emile. *Suicide*. Translated by John Spaulding and George Simpson. New York: Free Press, 1951.

Giovacchini, Peter. *The Urge To Die: Why Young People Commit Suicide*. New York: MacMillan, 1981.

Hendin, Herbert. *Suicide in America*. New York: Norton, 1982.

Klagsbrun, Francine. *Too Young to Die*. Boston: Houghton-Mifflin, 1976.

Mack, John, and Hickler, Holly. *Vivienne: The Life and Suicide of an Adolescent Girl*. Boston: Little, Brown, 1981.

McCoy, Kathleen. *Coping with Teenage Depression: A Parent's Guide*. New York: New American Library, 1982.

Saint-Exupery, Antoine de. *The Little Prince*. Translated by Katherine Woods. New York: Harcourt, Brace. 1969.

Hospitals, surgery, and illness can be traumatic for children, even under the best of circumstances. They can endure and survive the trauma better if they are well prepared.

Chapter Eight

Illness

Illness is never planned and therefore it can be a time of tremendous upheaval and turmoil for the family.

When a parent suddenly becomes ill, and especially if he is removed from the home, a child's world can collapse. Since the parent is usually the child's umbilical cord to life, having to survive without him, can be devastating.

The initial reaction of the child is sometimes shock, a numbness or seeming indifference. This can be mistaken for acceptance or apathy. It usually doesn't last long, however, and, frequently, disturbing changes in behavior shortly follow. The child may become terrified of being left and defiantly rebel at the suggestion of being in a room alone. It may take weeks and months for the child to return to his earlier level of behavior. Meanwhile, he needs the adults who care for him to understand and allow regressive behavior.

When the child himself is sick or faces a hospital experience, he can develop phobias that affect him for life. If the adults who love him, adequately prepare him, and stay nearby throughout the experience, the chances are greater that he will survive the ordeal with a minimum amount of trauma, quickly returning to age-appropriate behavior.

Child's Illness

Eric had been hospitalized for a relatively minor surgical procedure. Nevertheless, he was old enough and knew just enough to be very anxious about what would happen.

His mother, Bev, stayed with him the night before the operation. She and the medical personnel tried to prepare Eric for the experience by telling him exactly what would happen to him the next morning. Bev told him that he would experience some pain, but that she would stay with him until he went to sleep and would be there when he woke up. The nurses reassured Eric that his mother was telling the truth.

All went as planned and, when the medical personnel came to collect Eric for surgery, he willingly allowed them to wrap him in a green sheet and place him on the gurney. Bev accompanied him to the operating wing, but when they got to the pre-op area, she was told that she could go no farther. Suddenly, Eric was whisked off through the doors and Bev had to stay behind, without a chance to explain the change of procedure to her son or even tell him good-bye.

Eric was suddenly terrified. For the first time, he began crying for his mother, not able to understand why she had disappeared. He became tense and apprehensive, not knowing what to expect next. He had to lie on the gurney in the pre-op room, all alone, for over an hour, sobbing and scared, while his mother stood thirty feet down the hall, with tears of frustration and helplessness streaming down her face.

Eric was surprised to learn that what the adults had told him was wrong, and Bev, whom he had trusted completely, had deserted him. He went into surgery terrified, and came out the same way, thrashing under the anesthesia to the point where he dislodged the surgical packing and had to be further restrained.

Some of this anxiety could have been avoided. It was unfortunate that Bev had been led to believe that she would be allowed to stay with Eric until he fell asleep since it turned out that such was not the case. If Eric had been told the truth, he would have had time to get used to the idea, even if the thought was not a pleasant one. At least the credibility of the adults in charge would not have suffered. Undoubtedly, Eric would have been much calmer if he had not had to suffer abandonment at the last minute.

Hospitals, surgery, and illness can be traumatic for children, even under the best of circumstances. They can endure and survive the trauma better if they are well prepared. This involves being honest about procedures, pain, and separation. Children can deal with the known much better than they can with the unknown. We need to take the time necessary to prepare them adequately for the experiences—both pleasant and unpleasant—that they are going to have to face. At least, through it all, we will have kept our credibility intact and they will know that, whenever possible, we will deal with them honestly—even if the truth hurts.

It is estimated that over fifty percent of children have long-lasting difficulties stemming from the psychological trauma of minor surgery. Sometimes, the effects do not show up until months later in the form of residual fears and phobias.

Below the age of seven months, babies adjust quickly to new environments and people, and any changes in behavior appear to be brief.

After that age, however, the effects can be severe and long lasting. Frequently, the child becomes negative, demanding, and unreasonable. Sometimes he develops eating problems, sleep disturbances, separation anxiety, and resistance to authority, as well as panic over hospitals, falling, hurting himself, and sickness. Some become apathetic. Others withdraw.

Children of all ages seem to survive the ordeal of illness best when their parents room in and are able to stay with the child through the anesthesia induction.

Four-year-old Jason had been having recurring sore throats. Today he was running a fever and Lynn had kept him home.

"I think we had better go to see Dr. Morgan and see what he says," Lynn said at the breakfast table.

"He won't put me in the hospital, will he?"

"Why, Jason, why did you say that?"

"Because the last time I was there, he said that I might have to have my tonsils out. I don't want to have an operation."

"Well, I don't know. We'll just have to see."

Sure enough, Dr. Morgan, after taking a look at Jason's throat, said that he thought the time had come.

"We should just get this over with. I think I'd better schedule a tonsillectomy for you, Jason. How about next week?"

"Oh, no." Jason started crying. "I don't want to go in the hospital. No, No! Can't you just wait and see if I get better? I'll stay in bed."

"I'm sorry, Jason. You'll have to trust me. I'm the doctor, you know."

On the way home, Jason became hysterical. He cried and declared that he wouldn't go in the hospital, and he wouldn't let the doctor have his tonsils.

Lynn didn't know how in the world she was ever going to get him there.

Often, young children have misconceptions about illness, and hospitals. Sometimes they have picked these up from conversations, bits and pieces of which they misconstrue. For example, they feel that they may die, or lose their voice, or get stuck with a needle and lose all their blood, or have a throat or an arm or leg cut off.

Being this young and egocentric, they frequently blame themselves for an illness or need for an operation. They think they are having to pay for past sins—breaking a cup, throwing a tantrum.

They think they may never come back home or that their parents might forget them and leave them there.

They think they might go to sleep and never wake up.

They think their friends or siblings might forget them.

They think they might never be the same again, or that their friends might laugh at them.

They think the doctors and nurses might be very mean.

For a child who is going to enter the hospital, there are measures a parent can take to help alleviate his fears and minimize the negative effects such an experience might have for him:

- Talk with him honestly about everything that will happen to him. Role play as much as you can about what he will be experiencing. Use masks, needleless hypodermic syringes, stretchers, uniforms, and pretend medicines. It might also be helpful to draw a picture book for him using him as the central character showing all the things that are going to happen to him.

- Take him to the hospital and arrange for a visit through the children's ward if such is possible. Some hospitals have planned tours and will explain procedures and answer questions.

- Encourage him to take care of himself as much as possible. Help him to understand what and why certain procedures need to be done.

- Let him select favorite belongings to take with him (games, loveys, books, toys).

- Promise to stay with him as much as the hospital allows. Rooming-in is encouraged by most hospitals, and children fare much better when their parent stays with them.

- Treat the child as normally as possible. Don't make allowances and overindulge. The child who does not have limits feels even more insecure and nervous.

- Encourage your child to talk about his fears, perceptions and frustrations before he goes to the hospital and during the time he is there.

When he can verbalize these feelings, they will have much less effect on him in terms of psychosomatic symptoms and long-lasting effects.

- Read books about hospital experiences to him, i.e., *Curious George Goes to the Hospital* by Margaret and H. A. Rey, and *Elizabeth Gets Well* by Alfons Weber.

Admit your own feelings of doubt, fear, and anxiety to yourself. Seek some help and good listening from a trusted friend or understanding spouse. To a large extent, your child's reaction to the hospital stay will correlate with your own adjustment and coping skills.

A Parent's Illness

Marilyn, three, had begun to have night terrors. Although she used to stay in her bed and sleep through the night, she was now waking up every few hours and screaming for her mother.

The past few months had been rocky for Marilyn. Three months before, her mother, Joanne, who had been suffering from severe headaches, had suddenly been admitted to the hospital for tests. Three days later, she had been flown to the Mayo Clinic where she had undergone brain surgery. Joanne and her husband were gone for a month. Marilyn had stayed with her grandmother. When Joanne had returned home, she had to lie flat on her back for two weeks with her head bandaged.

It was not until a month later that Marilyn had begun to have night terrors.

Of course, Joanne and Rick were sympathetic, but they were exhausted from their trying experience and didn't know how to deal with their child's unreasonable demands. They sought help from a wise and understanding friend and followed through on their friend's suggestion: they got a loose–leaf notebook and on the cover, wrote, *"Marilyn's Story."*

Inside they wrote, "Once upon a time, there was a family whose name was Calvin. They were a very happy family. Daddy, Mama, and Marilyn, who was three years old, lived in a pretty house and did many fun things together. They liked to ride bikes, play ball and go to the beach."

Joanne drew pictures to illustrate. She also pasted in some photographs of the three of them.

"One day, Mommy got a bad headache. She was very sick. She went to bed but her headache didn't get any better. She called the doctor, and he told Mommy to come to see him. When he examined her head, the doctor said that she would have to go to the hospital."

"Mommy came home to get her nightgown, slippers, robe, and toothbrush and to tell Marilyn 'good-by.' She kissed her and told her that she was going to the hospital, but that Daddy would bring Marilyn to see her each day. Marilyn and Mommy were sad." Pictures were drawn showing Joanne hugging Marilyn and both of them wearing sad faces.

"Mommy was in the hospital three days. Daddy brought Marilyn to see Mommy each day. Mommy got to hug Marilyn and to read a story to her.

"Then, the doctor said that Mommy would have to have an operation. She would have to fly away on a big plane and go to a big hospital. Daddy said that he would go with Mommy and that Marilyn would stay at Grandma's."

"Marilyn came to the hospital to tell Mommy and Daddy goodbye. Everyone was sad." (Many sad faces!) "Mommy and Daddy flew on a big plane and Marilyn went to stay at Grandma's. (Here, a picture of an airplane, a big house, the hospital, and a picture of Marilyn at Grandma's, baking cookies, playing with the dog, taking walks.)

"Sometimes Marilyn felt sad and lonely. Sometimes she forgot, because her friends came and took her out. She got to go lots of places."

"Marilyn and her Mommy missed each other very much." (Sad faces.)

"Mommy had her operation and the doctor fixed her headaches. Mommy had many flowers around her bed. She still missed Marilyn. Mommy talked with Marilyn on the telephone almost every day. Sometimes they both cried." (More pictures.)

"Finally one day the doctor said that Mommy could come home. She and Daddy were so happy. They brought presents for Marilyn."

"Grandma took Marilyn to the airport to meet Mommy and Daddy. They had big smiles on their faces when they saw each other. They hugged and kissed Marilyn lots of times. They even brought balloons."

"When they got home, Mommy had to stay in bed with a big scarf around her head. Marilyn could come in the room to see Mommy, but she had to tiptoe and talk quietly. It was a little scary to see Mommy in bed with a big scarf on her head."

"In several weeks, Mommy could get out of bed. She sat on the sofa and read many books to Marilyn."

"Mommy and Marilyn were so happy to be back together again. Daddy was happy too."

"The Calvin family was together again."

(Many pictures of happy faces. Some more photographs.)

Once Joanne finished making the book, she showed it to Marilyn.

She told her that she had a very special book for her and she wanted to read it to her. If she wanted to, Marilyn could draw more pictures in it as they went along.

Joanne read the story to her child.

Marilyn started crying.

"Why are you crying? Does it make you sad?" Joanne gently asked Marilyn.

The child nodded.

Joanne said, "Were you worried?"

"Yes."

"What were you worried about?"

"I was worried because you didn't take your boots."

"Were you worried that my feet would get cold?"

"Yes."

"Were you afraid?"

"Yes."

"What were you afraid of?"

"That you wouldn't ever come back—and then who would take care of me?"

When they got to the picture of the airplane showing Joanne and Rick coming home, Marilyn wanted to draw their faces in the window.

She wanted to draw flowers around Joanne's bed after she got home too.

After Joanne had finished reading the book, Marilyn immediately wanted to hear it again, and again. It became her favorite book and she wanted to hear it many times a day. She carried it around with her, and sometimes she sat and read it to herself.

Joanne could hear her saying, "Marilyn was very sad. She felt like crying. It's all right. Your Mommy is coming back."

About two weeks later, Marilyn's desire to have the book read to her subsided. It still was one of her favorites but not the only one she wanted to hear. About that time, her night terrors disappeared also.

A child must be given an opportunity to express what is bothering her. Her very own book is an excellent way to accomplish this.

Hospital/Illness

For children ages 4 to 8:

Rey, Margaret and Hans Rey. *Curious George Goes to the Hospital*. Boston: Houghton Mifflin Co., 1966. Fiction.

> This entertaining book depicts a common hospital experience, including illustrations of wheelchairs, x-ray machines, and operating rooms.

Sharmat, Marjorie Weinman. *I Want Mama*. New York: Harper and Row Publishers, 1974. Fiction.

> This story describes the loneliness, anxiety, and anger experienced by a young child when a parent enters the hospital for several days.

Sobol, Helen L. *Jeff's Hospital Book*. New York: Henry Z. Walck, 1975. Nonfiction.

> A sensitive story about a young boy having eye surgery. This book presents accurate information and examines the boy's feelings and fears.

Sonneborn, Ruth A. *I Love Gram*. New York: The Viking Press, 1971. Fiction.

> The story illustrates the love a little girl feels for her grandmother. It is helpful for a child who has a close relative in the hospital.

Stein, Sara Bonnett. *A Hospital Story: An Open Family Book for Parents and Children Together*. New York: Walker and Co., 1974. Nonfiction.

A realistic portrayal of the experiences surrounding a young girl's hospitalization for a tonsillectomy.

For children ages 8 to 12:

Kay, Eleanor. *The Emergency Room*. New York: Franklin Watts, Inc., 1970. Nonfiction.

This book describes the experiences of an eleven-year-old boy who is admitted to a hospital emergency room after a serious accident.

Singer, Marilyn. *It Can't Hurt Forever*. New York: Harper and Row Publishers, 1978. Fiction.

This first-person narrative is filled with candid observations concerning serious surgery and lengthy hospital stays.

For children ages 12 to 16:

Lowry, Lois. *A Summer to Die*. Boston: Houghton Mifflin Co., 1977. Fiction.

This book portrays the warmth of both family life and friendships. A sibling's illness and death are described with touching realism.

For adults:

McCollum, Audrey T. *The Chronically Ill Child*. New Haven: The Yale University Press, 1975. Nonfiction.

A thoughtful, practical guide for parents. The book covers the problems and reactions of disabled children of various age levels and of the parents who are trying to help them.

Every new skill mastered enhances self esteem.

Chapter Nine

Children Who Are Different

All of us expect and hope that our children will be normal. When they are not, additional stress is immediately placed on the family. Help is needed.

There is a tendency for parents of children with problems to make exceptions for them—to treat them with partiality without realizing it—and to make them more handicapped than they already are.

The reasons for this mistake are numerous and complicated. Sometimes the parents blame themselves for the child's condition. Sometimes they resent the added burden and compensate for their guilt by spoiling the child and not requiring enough from him. Sometimes they bury their own identity into that of the child and become accustomed to the martyr role. To give it up would be to lose their own identity.

Whatever the reason, parents of children who are different need to understand the importance of helping their child to become as independent and socially acceptable as possible. They also need to work hard to keep life in perspective and not allow the needs of their special child to overshadow the rights and privileges of other family members to whom they are responsible.

Physical Handicaps

A year ago, on a Saturday in July, George, four, started complaining of a headache. Anna took his temperature and found that he had a fever of 101°. That night, he was nauseated, but the next day he seemed to feel better. Sunday night, he again became lethargic and threw up before bedtime.

His parents decided to call the doctor in the morning if George didn't feel better. Early the next morning, his parents found him crying and complaining of a stiff neck. When they tried to get him up, he kept falling.

Alarmed, they called the pediatrician who met them at the hospital.

A few hours later, they were told that George had meningitis. The illness left him with a severe hearing loss.

Up until that time, he had been a delightful, happy-go-lucky child who made friends easily.

However, during the last year, life had changed for George. Not only had it been necessary for him to adjust to wearing hearing aids, but he had also had to learn when and how to put them in and take them out.

He had been the center of much attention. His parents and other relatives had felt desperately sorry for him and had tried to protect him from harm, danger, curious children, and inquisitive adults.

They had begun to notice that George's personality was changing from that of an agreeable, content little boy to an aggressive, whining, demanding, and unpleasant child.

George had learned to swim before his illness, so Anna took him to the neighborhood pool every day. She was careful to remind him to remove his hearing aids before getting in the pool.

One day at the pool, George was on the diving board when the lifeguard blew his whistle. Naturally, George didn't hear the warning, so he proceeded to dive in the pool.

Different

124

Ann was embarrassed and ran to get George out of the pool. Helping him out, she explained to him that the lifeguard had blown the whistle. Then, she went to the lifeguard to tell him that he would have to remember that George was deaf, and he would have to get his attention another way when it was time for the children to get out of the pool.

The lifeguard didn't feel that it should be his responsibility to keep up with George. He felt that he had enough responsibility watching the other children.

Anna told him if he couldn't look after George, she wasn't going to be able to bring him to the pool anymore.

Angry and frustrated, Anna took George home.

Although it is very natural for Anna to feel sorry for her son, she is not doing him any favors by trying to get other people to become responsible for his safety.

George needs to learn survival skills. In this particular instance, he could be taught that each time he starts to go in the pool, he first needs to look at the lifeguard and make sure that he is not calling for time out.

George needs to learn how to get along in a world where other people can hear. He will quickly develop compensatory strategies to cope with his disability. As long as Anna takes care of him and looks out for him, he will not feel the necessity of learning coping and survival skills.

It would be helpful if his parents would treat George, as much as possible, in the same way they did before his illness. They need to remember that he is a child first and a disabled child second. If George gets special privileges because of his handicap, he will fail to learn necessary coping devices and will lose his wonderful ability to role with the punches, adapt to the wishes and needs of other children, and learn from facing the consequences of his behavior.

Twelve-year-old Steve had never been a problem at school except that his teachers complained of his daydreaming. They had constantly reported to his parents that Steve "could do better," if he would just pay attention.

Mrs. Ferry, his fifth grade teacher, having just read an article on epilepsy, was the first one to be suspicious that there might be something wrong with Steve. She mentioned it to the school nurse, who suggested that the parents be advised to take him to a neurologist.

Naturally his parents were distressed to learn that Steve might have a physical problem. They made an appointment right away.

After giving the child an EEG, the neurologist confirmed the fact that Steve did actually have a form of epilepsy and told them that he could have been having as many as 15 to 20 absence (petit mal) seizures every day. He explained to them that this form of epilepsy is not as obvious as tonic-clonic (grand mal) seizures which result in falling on the floor, stiffness and jerking.

Steve's parents were shocked. They immediately began to read and research everything they could find on epilepsy. Feeling sorry for Steve, they began to curtail his activities and control his environment so that he would not encounter any dangerous situations.

When they told their relatives about Steve's problem, the parents were hurt by their insensitive and unenlightened responses: "Is it contagious?" "Let's keep it a secret." "Other people won't want him around." "I think we'll cancel out on keeping him for a week this summer like we had promised. Suppose he had a seizure?" "He will probably never marry." "What will he be able to do?" "Can he finish school?" "Will he be able to drive a car?"

As Steve's parents became more and more hostile, angry and defeated, they tended to overprotect their son. Since he didn't seem to be able to remember when to take his medicine, they put themselves in charge. They inhibited him from many of the activities which he enjoyed—afraid that he would suffer from embarrassment and ridicule.

If Steve's parents do not change their attitudes about their son's disability, they could make him an emotional cripple.

Steve needs to become responsible for taking his own medication. He needs to be told in clear terms by his neurologist exactly what his limitations are. Relatives and friends also need to be told what epilepsy really is and how it affects a child. Once others are enlightened, they can be much more realistic and helpful, and Steve will learn to live his own life and be able to accept his limitations as well as forge on, as all of us must do, to make the most of our capabilities and opportunities.

Mental Handicaps

Carolyn and Mark were expecting their first child. Carolyn had tried for two years to get pregnant, so naturally they were ecstatic.

Mark had gone to the Lamaze classes with Carolyn, and together they had furnished the baby's room, complete with clothes, diapers, mobiles, stuffed animals, rattles, blankets, and cradle.

Finally, the big day arrived. Carolyn woke up with labor pains, they called the doctor and left for the hospital as soon as he said it was necessary.

The labor was a long one, and Carolyn was exhausted. The doctor decided on a caesarean. He suggested that Mark might not want to stay in the delivery room.

It seemed like hours before anyone came to tell Mark anything.

When they did, he knew something was wrong.

"You have a boy, Mr. Long."

"Is he all right?"

"No, I'm afraid there are some complications. We won't know for awhile. We will have to put him on a life support system. We will hope for the best."

When a new baby enters the world, there is an adjustment for any family to make. Usually the joys of watching a healthy, bright, and beautiful baby change and grow in a miraculous way compensates for the demands, the sleepless nights, and the inconveniences which the whole family experiences. However, when that baby is sick or imperfect, hopes and dreams are shattered and the usual joy and pleasant challenge shift suddenly to fear and despair. Perhaps the family is not aware of "differentness" until sometime later, but whenever the realization comes, there is a big adjustment which must be made. Families of "special" children need a great deal of understanding, help, and support.

Even if the specialness or handicap manifests itself later, the families have a terrific adjustment to make.

There are certain stages which most families pass through before they can fully accept their "special" child and be able to deal constructively with the problems and decisions they will face.

1. *Denial* is the first stage most parents experience. They cannot accept the reality of the situation and, at best, want to minimize the severity of the problem.

2. *Blame* is the next common reaction. Most people want to find someone who is responsible for the trouble (physician, hospital, self, or spouse's family).

3. *Fear* of the unknown comes next. The parents wonder what caused the trouble, will other children be affected, what is their future with this child, how will friends and relatives react, how expensive will the care be, who will look after the child when they are no longer able?

4. *Guilt* often follows closely behind. What did we do to deserve this? Why us? Is it a payment for past sins?

5. *Mourning or grief* are natural reactions to situations which bring extreme pain and disappointment. When parents become aware that their child will never fulfill their expectations and lead a normal life, the child of their dreams ceases to exist and parents grieve and mourn as if the child had actually died. Many parents experience death wishes for their "special" child, sometimes consciously, sometimes not.

6. *Withdrawal* is a natural next step in the long road to acceptance. It takes time alone for most people to work out their feelings, analyze and plan for the future. Some people no longer want to be with their friends.

7. *Rejection* often comes before acceptance. It can take many forms. Some parents underestimate the child's potential, while others set unrealistically high goals. Some people try to escape. They may take on extra jobs or find ways to be busy on weekends. Still others develop a facade of "nothing but love" for the child. They deny all their negative feelings and try to be "perfect" parents.

8. *Acceptance* is the final step in the long and difficult adjustment which the family must make. When this acceptance has occurred, the family is able to value the child as a person with feelings and needs like other children., They realize that he has potential to enjoy life and to bring enjoyment to others. They are able to set realistic, attainable goals for him that can bring satisfaction, pleasure, and pride. After traveling through the pain, frustration, and self-doubts, parents can emerge stronger, knowing that not only have they endured a major crisis but that they have grown into wiser and more compassionate human beings as well.

Nan had taken nine-year-old Susie who has Down's Syndrome, with her to do her weekly grocery shopping. As usual, she tried to involve her daughter in the event. When they got to the cookies, Nan selected two different kinds and told Susie that she could choose one of them.

"I want both," cried Susie.

"No, Susie," Nan patiently told her. "You may have only one."

Susie got louder. "Both!" and threw both boxes on the floor.

Trying to remain calm, Nan was picking the cookies up when a shopper, who had been standing nearby, came over to them. "You ought to go ahead and give her both boxes. What can it hurt? After all, the child is going to have a rough enough time in life without having to put up with more hassles from you. Poor thing. She's retarded, isn't she? She's so sweet. Give her the cookies."

Nan was upset with the shopper and the scene that Susie had created. Reluctantly, she gave in and let Susie have both boxes of cookies.

Nan allowed the opinion of a stranger to discourage her from carrying out the discipline techniques which she felt were best.

Parents of retarded children spend most of their lives tired and lonely. Their children require more of everything than other children do—and there are just twenty-four hours in a day.

No one, except the parents of another handicapped child, could possibly know the extra amount of effort it takes to "live normally"—to talk to neighbors, shop for groceries, attend P.T.A., take children to the doctor, entertain friends, drive the car pool—when you must somehow squeeze in the extraordinary care a disabled child requires.

Other disruptions—the birth of a baby, the illness or death of a family member—are temporary and society knows how to respond with attention, hot meals, cards, visits, until the family has had time to recover, regroup, and go on. However, no one expects friends and family to respond endlessly to a crisis that never ends.

At first, these parents try bravely to meet the demands of everyday life. They expend enormous amounts of energy trying to be good parents, attend meetings, volunteer, take their little ones in tow, trying to look confident while anticipating the hurdles: the grocery carts, the swinging doors, the stairs, and the unkind comments and the thoughtless remarks. They read everything they can get their hands on and follow every lead—on specialists, training, cures, schools, *help!*

Then, reality sets in. This problem is not going to get solved. Friends and family slowly drift away. They no longer mention the tragedy. There is less and less to talk about. The demands of the child take the family farther and farther away from the mainstream of life.

By the time the child is a teenager, the life-style has definitely changed. Most families, by this time, have stripped their lives to the bare essentials. They no longer try to live like other people. They don't think in terms of recreation, fun, trips, "going out." The physical and psychic energy expenditure has taken its toll. They have settled for never being "normal" again.

> Randy, 19, had grown up in the neighborhood and the neighbors had grown accustomed to his ways. He frequently rode his bicycle recklessly down the street, pestered the children, or shouted wildly at a friend a half a block away.
>
> Van and Carol had tried their best to teach him the rules of society, but they couldn't watch him every minute. Many times they were embarrassed by his behavior.
>
> A new neighbor moved in two doors away. Being neighborly, Carol and Randy greeted them with a pie the first week they were there. Carol tried to explain about Randy and added that if he ever became a nuisance, to be sure to let her know.
>
> A week later, the new neighbor was at the door. When Carol greeted her, she started in, "Do you realize how dangerous it is for Randy to ride his bicycle on the street? He could get killed. I watched him today weaving in and out of traffic. I don't want to be the one that hits him. And then he came visiting us and scared my little girl to death. I think you should keep him home or put him in an institution. He is a menace to society. I'm going

to report you. I think it is shameful that you don't keep an eye on him. If he were mine, I would look after him."

Carol was devastated and embarrassed. All she could say was, "I'm sorry he bothered you. I will talk to him about it. Sometimes I just don't know what to do with him." She started crying.

Other people can be so quick to make judgments when the "special child" belongs to someone else! These parents need support and understanding more than any other kinds of parents.

There *are* things others can do:

- Most of all, be sensitive and never make judgments about how others handle their "special" child. If you haven't walked in their moccasins, you don't know how they fit.

- Offer practical help—to child sit while the parents grocery shop, or attend parent–support groups, or go to the movies, or spend time alone. Offer to take the child for a walk, a ride, or to the park, so the parents can have a few hours or responsibility-free time.

- Remember that people with handicapping conditions are more normal than abnormal. They have the same basic needs that the rest of us have—to be loved, accepted, and taught to be as socially adept as possible.

- Their parents' needs are normal too: to be commended for putting up with overwhelming problems most of us know nothing about, and to be respected as first class citizens who need help and understanding.

Society is a long way away from being ready to deal with our retarded members and their families. Until we become knowledgeable, sensitive, and accepting, we will continue to force them into lives of fatigue and loneliness as well as fail to give to them the support they deserve.

Siblings of the Handicapped

When Jan was three years old, she contracted German measles. Betty, who was pregnant at the time, tried to stay away from her daughter, but Jan didn't understand. She whined and begged her mother to read to her at night before going to bed.

When Jan's little sister, Alicia, was born deaf, Betty was distraught. She even explained to Jan that the reason her little sister couldn't hear was because she had caught the German measles from her while she was still in Mommy's tummy.

Jan didn't understand.

As she got older, however, she was reminded many times that she was the cause of her sister's deafness. When she complained about inconveniences caused by her sister's handicap, she was quickly reminded that if it hadn't been for her, Alicia would be able to hear.

Jan grew up feeling guilty. She wished that she had been the one who was deaf. Then her mother would love her, hold her, rock her, and give her special attention and love.

When Jan finished high school and wanted to go to college, she was told that since they had had to spend extra money for Alicia's schooling, they didn't have enough left for her.

Because children who are special take so much of their parents' time, concern, and energy, it would be easy to overlook the needs of the other children in the home.

The questions listed below were devised to give families a vehicle to use to stimulate conversation between family members and, it is hoped, open up discussion about important matters which may have been difficult to talk about.

When asking the questions, the word "different" should be changed to that of handicapped, retarded, deaf, exceptional, special, or whatever word applies. The wording should suit the age and understanding of the child.

- Do you ever feel guilty because you are not "different" and your brother/sister is?

- Are you ever embarrassed to bring friends to your house because they might see your "different" brother/sister?

- Are you ever embarrassed to tell your friends that you have a "different" brother/sister?

- When you play with your "different" brother/sister and he/she accidently hits his/her head or is bruised, are you ever afraid that the accident could cause further problems or complications?

- Do you understand the cause of your brother's/sister's problem/ "differentness?"

- Do your parents spend more time with your "different" brother/ sister than with you?

- Do you feel that you are denied material possessions or family vacations because of the cost of the medical treatment for your brother/sister?

- Are you ever concerned about the future for your brother/sister and how it could affect your future?

- Do your parents ever ask your advice on decisions regarding your brother/sister?

- Do you ever wonder why your brother/sister is "different" and you are not?

- Do you feel that having a "different" brother/sister has made you more understanding/compassionate and aware of the world's less fortunate people?

- Do you ever feel neglected/jealous of the amount of time and attention your parents must give to your "different" brother/ sister?

- Because your parents must spend a great deal of time with your "different" brother/sister, do you ever feel the need to be especially "good" or to excel in some manner to attract the attention of your parents and get their approval?

- Do you ever feel pressure to become more successful because you know that your brother/sister will not be able to achieve the goals that you can?

- Do you ever resent the amount of time you have to care for your brother/sister when you could be doing something else?

- Do your parents ever make you include your brother/sister in your plans with your friends?

When children are exposed early in life to others who are less fortunate and require extra care, they often develop extra sensitivity which stays with them for life. This is one reason that "mainstreaming" has proven to be so successful, not only for the child who has special problems, but for the other children in the classroom who are exposed to the "differentness" at an early age. They frequently gain an awareness and acceptance which some people never seem to develop.

Many siblings of children who are "different" grow up feeling special themselves and show their compassion and gratitude by choosing careers in which they devote their time and energy to helping those who are less fortunate. It is important to remember that the way all children are treated when they are young will determine to a large extent the feelings they will have for themselves and others throughout their entire lifetimes.

Handicapped

For children ages 4 to 8:
Petersen, Palle. *Sally Can't See*. New York: John Day Co., 1977.
Nonfiction.
Sally is not strange, only blind, and this teaches children not to treat blind people artificially or patronizingly.

Peterson, Jeanne. *I Have A Sister—My Sister Is Deaf*. New York: Harper & Row Publishers, 1977. Fiction.
In telling about her deaf sister, a hearing girl shows the way in which a deaf child differs from a hearing one.

Pursell, Margaret Sanford. *A Look At Physical Handicaps*. Lerner Publications Co., 1976. Nonfiction.
This book shows that someone who is different is not an oddity.

For children ages 8 to 12:

Brown, Patricia. *Someone Special, Just Like You*. New York: Holt, Rinehart & Winston, 1984. Nonfiction.
This book shows disabled children who like to swim, paint, and do a host of other things that able-bodied children like to do.

Garrigue, Sheila. *Between Friends*. Scarsdale, NY: Bradbury Press, Inc., 1978. Fiction.
This sensitive story explores the fears and prejudice that often surround mentally handicapped people.

Smith, Doris Buchanan. *Kelly's Creek*. New York: Thomas Y. Crowell Co., 1975. Fiction.
A vigorous little boy with a learning disability gains the self-respect he desperately deserves.

Sobol, Harriet L. *My Brother Steven Is Retarded*. New York: Macmillan Publishing Co., 1977. Fiction.
This first-person narrative follows a girl's exploration of her mixed feelings toward her retarded brother.

For children ages 12 to 16:

Albert, Louise. *But I'm Ready To Go*. Scarsdale, NY: Bradbury Press, 1976. Fiction.
This story, written to an imaginary friend by an intelligent, sensitive girl with a learning disability, includes much about the rejection and inadequacy felt by people with such handicaps.

Cook, Marjorie. *To Walk On Two Feet*. Philadelphia, PA: The Westminster Press, 1978. Fiction.
The disablement, anger, and depression a teenage amputee feels are vividly portrayed in this book.

For adults:

Cunningham, Cliff and Patricia Sloper. *Helping Your Exceptional Baby*. New York: Pantheon Books, 1978. Nonfiction.
This book is filled with straightforward advice, developmental checklists, and ideas for the stimulation and teaching of exceptional children.

Greenfeld, Josh. *A Place For Noah*. New York: Washington Square Press, 1978. Nonfiction.
A first hand account of a family's struggle to make a place for their brain-damaged son.

Spock, Benjamin and Marion Lerrigo. *Caring For Your Disabled Child*. New York: Macmillan Books, 1967. Nonfiction.
A comprehensive book for parents with a child who is blind, deaf, crippled, or in any way handicapped. It also contains a useful annotated bibliography to which parents may turn for further help in understanding their child and his particular disability.

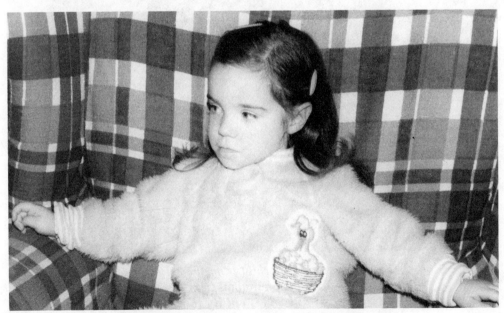

Because children who are special take so much of their parents' time, concern, and energy, it would be easy to overlook the needs of the other children in the home.

Be honest with your child from the very begin-
ning. If he feels his family has been living a lie,
he could lose faith in his ability to trust you.

Chapter Ten

Adoption

When adults are unable to have children of their own, they often consider adoption. Even though this is a viable option for them, the risks involved are many.

It often takes a long time to be approved for legal adoption through an agency. There is a period of investigation, endless personal questions, and unbearable waiting. There are the inevitable risks: the genetic background of the child, the health and personality of the child, the child's future acceptance or rejection of the adoptive parents, and the family's adjustment to the child.

Once the child has been adopted, if it is a baby, there is the question of when, how, and if to tell him his life story. If the child is older, the period of adjustment is often trying, lengthy, discouraging, and full of testing. The more disruption the child has suffered in the past (foster homes, abuse, rejection), the longer and harder the adjustment period will be.

Families need to be aware of the possible pitfalls before they commit themselves to adoption. Although the road may be long and rocky, it can turn into a beautiful, rewarding experience for all involved.

When and How to Tell a Child

Terri, 6, came running in the house to tell her mother that Janet, 8, was crying in the swing, because she said that Terri wasn't her "real" sister.

Shocked, Susan dropped what she was doing and went outside to find Janet. Sure enough, the child was sitting in the swing crying.

"What's wrong, Janet? Why are you crying?"

The child kept crying but wouldn't answer.

Susan prodded, "What did you tell Terri?"

The little sister, who had tagged along, volunteered, "She said I wasn't her *real* sister—that she is adopted."

"Who told you that, Janet? Where did you hear that?" Susan asked.

"Barbie told her today while she was babysitting." Terri answered for her sister, who had stopped crying, but was staring at the ground.

Susan sat down beside Janet and lifted Terri into her lap.

"Barbie had no business telling you that. I was going to tell you myself when I though you were old enough, but, yes, she is right. You *were* adopted, Janet, but that doesn't mean that Terri isn't your 'real' sister. Of course she is your 'real' sister, and I am your 'real' mother. 'Adopted' means that you didn't grow in my tummy, but you have always been my little girl, and I love you just as much as I would if you *had* grown in my tummy."

"Am *I* adopted? Did *I* grow in your tummy?" Terri asked.

"Yes, Terri, you grew in my tummy. No, you weren't adopted but I love you both the same. Some day soon, Daddy and I will tell you the whole story."

Janet started crying again and Susan put her arm around her.

"Don't cry," she said, not knowing what else to say.

Most adoptive parents worry about how and when (and if) to tell their children they were adopted. There doesn't seem to be a *best* time or way to break this news to a child.

Some people use the word "adopted" from the very beginning, so that the child will be used to hearing it and not suffer trauma from hearing it for the first time when he is older.

Other parents wait until they think the child is old enough to understand, and still others don't ever tell. This latter decision sometimes backfires when a child is rummaging through dresser drawers and stumbles on adoption papers, or, in rare cases, doesn't find out until the parents die and they need to read legal documents.

Most authorities agree that when a child finds out on his own, he is likely to suffer severe trauma (an abnormal life experience) as opposed to distress (a normal life experience). The child may feel his family has been living a lie, and he will lose faith in his ability to trust them.

It is ideal if the parents agree from the very beginning to answer all questions honestly when they are asked. This seems to be the safest and easiest way to tell a child that he is adopted. The rule of thumb is never to lie to a child. (Keeping secrets in a family is usually dangerous.) Your only obligation is to answer the questions the child asks, however, and while he is young, these can be answered quite simply.

It is important to agree on the terminology which suits you. It is probably best to avoid "real" or "natural," since the opposites are "unreal" and "unnatural." The term "birth mother" might prove to be a useful alternative.

When other people ask difficult questions such as, "Where did she get red hair?" a simple statement such as, "Red hair runs in the family," will suffice. If they thoughtlessly ask innane questions such as, "Isn't it harder to love your adopted child," you might answer, "What makes you ask such a question?"

Remember that a young child can only "take in" so much information. He will have to be told his story many times before it sinks in. A scrapbook entitled, "Your Story" with pictures depicting the first days, weeks, and years of living in the family—can help make the story real. Most children love to hear stories about the "first night" when the phone rang off the hook and all the neighbors dropped by to see the baby.

At certain points, children will ask questions or make statements that the parents don't want to hear, such as, "I wish I had grown in your tummy." The best way to respond is with honesty, "I wish you had grown in my tummy, too, but you didn't."

Children can handle the truth. It is deception that causes trouble.

Parental Expectations

"Huh? No, I don't know. Yeah. O.K. Mother, telephone!" Penny, 8, yelled to Kathy, her mother.

"Penny, why did you yell? Why didn't you come get me?" Kathy complained, as she took the receiver. It was Penny's grandmother on the phone.

"Honestly, Kathy, you need to teach that child some manners. She was so rude, I wanted to hang up the phone. What's wrong with her? I know you've taught her better than that."

"I know, Mom. I'm embarrassed at the way she talks to my friends, too. I don't know what to do about it. I've talked until I'm blue in the face."

"Well, Janice doesn't seem to have any trouble with Sue, and Sue is younger than Penny. You should hear Sue on the phone. She's so polite. She makes you glad you called. She always sounds so pleasant."

Kathy felt discouraged and defeated. "Honestly, Mother. I try. I can't be perfect. It hurts my feelings when anyone criticizes her."

"Well I didn't mean to hurt your feelings. You do a wonderful job with her. Of course, she isn't perfect. I think you are especially sensitive since she is not yours. It's probably easier to see faults and to correct children when they are your flesh and blood. Maybe you want everyone to think you are a perfect mother, and that's why it gets to you."

Kathy thought a minute. "Probably so, Mom." She felt like crying.

After talking with her mother a few more minutes, she hung up. She felt confused and didn't want to talk with Penny about it. She went to her room. Why did she try so hard to be a supermom?

One of the pitfalls that adoptive parents can fall into is that of trying too hard to be perfect parents. At an unconscious level, they may feel the need to prove that they are worthy of having a child and that the child is lucky to have them.

It is hard on adults to accept the fact that they are unable to reproduce, and at some level, they probably feel somewhat defeated perhaps even inferior. This underlying feeling could cause them to over-compensate by trying to be superparents. This means making an effort to correct every mistake on the one hand, but never to hurt the child's feelings, on the other—an impossible bind.

Children need limits. They need to be taught manners, responsibility, and socially accepted behavior. At times, parents have to endure their child's wrath and hurt feelings, for growth and maturity often result from pain and painful experiences. Parents will not always be popular, and adoptive parents may have a harder time than most accepting this reality.

Adolescence

Tammy had been told since she was a baby that she was adopted. At the time her parents told her that "adopted" meant "special." They told her that most parents had to take what they got, but they had been able to choose her. That made her very special. When she had been a little girl, that had seemed to satisfy her.

Although the grandparents used to "whisper" about her being adopted, her parents did not hesitate to talk about it openly to her and to all their friends and relatives. They used to be very provoked with the "old-fashioned" grandparents who continued to whisper.

However, by the time Tammy reached adolescence, she no longer wanted to feel "special," because "special" meant "different" and she wanted very much to be like everybody else.

Her parents noticed that she was becoming very withdrawn and sullen. They talked with a child psychologist who suggested that they might need to talk again with Tammy about her adoption. He explained that as children got older and were able to figure things out, they often had new thoughts about their heritage and sometimes carried misconceptions into adulthood, because they didn't want to talk about it for fear of hurting their parents.

Her mother decided to talk with Tammy about it. "You've seemed sort of sad lately. I wonder if perhaps we could have a talk."

The child seemed uninterested at first, but her mother continued, "I wonder if you have been thinking about the fact that you are adopted. Has it been bothering you? I know that when you were little, we used to talk a lot about it, but since you have grown up, we hardly ever discuss it. Do you have any questions you would like to ask?

"Well, I have been thinking a lot about it lately. At school, we have a new girl, and the other girls have been whispering that they heard she was adopted. They sort of say the word like she has cancer or something. I don't know whether they remember that I'm adopted or not, but they talk funny about her. They say she's 'illegitimate.' I'm afraid they'll make fun of me too," said Tammy.

She went on, "Why *did* my mother give me away? You always told me I was special. If I was so special, why did she give me away? Didn't she like me? I bet if I lived with her now, she would like me better than you do. All you do is fuss with me. I bet she wouldn't fuss. I wish I could have a chance to see her and maybe live with her."

Of course, her mother felt hurt, but she tried to hold back the tears. "It's natural for you to think about her, Tammy. I've told you all I know about her, but I will tell you again." She repeated the facts that she had related many times before.

This time, the child seemed to hold on to every word. "Do you know what she looked like? What would my name be? Did she play tennis? Why didn't she want to keep me?"

"Tammy, she was only 17 years old and she wasn't married. You know your baby sitter is 17 years old. Can you imagine her with a baby?"

Tammy shook her head.

"You see, she was so young and trying to take care of a baby would have meant that she wouldn't have been able to finish school. I'm sure it was hard for her to give you up, but she felt that you would have a better home with us. I'm certainly glad she did, for you have brought us so much happiness."

"Can I ever see her?"

"When you are grown, if you want to look her up, you can try."

"I don't want to talk about it any more. Leave me alone," Tammy suddenly said to her mother.

When children reach adolescence, there is a developmental need to search for their identity. In order to accomplish this difficult and all-important task, a psychological disengagement from their parents is necessary. This manifests itself in the child's withdrawing emotionally, often retreating to his room for long hours, talking on the telephone and giving curt and short answers to parents.

This is an especially hard time for children who are adopted. In order to know who you are, it is helpful to find clues from your past. One of the ways we do this is to look at our parents and examine their physical characteristics, their interests, strengths, needs, likes and dislikes, beliefs, values, and political and religious tenets.

Ideally, the child will emerge from adolescence with a strong sense of identity and "connectedness" as well as a sense of independence. This developmental task is difficult for children who never knew their birth parents. If they are not given the facts, they often fantasize about their past.

When adoptive parents seem uninterested in answering the child's questions or give them scanty information, the child often interprets this as indifference to him, or worse, that he was not worth your bothering to find out about his background, or that his parents were so bad you don't want him to know. These assumptions can lead to even more trouble for the struggling adolescent.

When there is not free and open communication between adoptive parents and their children, the child often feels a sense of incompleteness that can affect his happiness, coping skills, and ability to move through this difficult developmental stage.

However, when parents have always answered the questions honestly, children emerge from adolescence having resolved many of the issues which at one time loomed so large and having accepted the facts of their lives over which they have no control.

Although the increased questioning on their child's part often strikes fear in the hearts of the adoptive parents, if they are patient and keep their hurt feelings to themselves, they will find that the child will most likely come around to feeling love and appreciation for all that has been done for him.

Sometimes children this age will derive some comfort from writing to members of the Adoptee Pen Pal Club and sharing concerns with others who find themselves in the same situation.

Melissa's parents had adopted her when she was eight years old. She had been taken away from her mother when she was 2 because she had been abused. When she was naughty, her mother used to tie kerosene-soaked rags around her ankles and set them on fire. Finally, the authorities took the children away and put them in foster homes. Her brothers and sisters had been placed together, but she was shifted from one foster home to another. Her current family was the first to want to adopt her.

At first, she had worn their patience thin. She had lied, taken things that weren't hers, run away several times, and gotten in many fights at school. One day when she got mad at her mother, she went to her room, locked the door, and started playing with matches. Before long, she had set her room on fire and had come close to suffocating herself in the fire.

Her parents were distraught. The social worker had explained that because of Melissa's background, she would have to do a lot of testing. They would have to be patient. . .but for how long?

They never dreamed that she would set fire to their house. They wondered if they had made a mistake by adopting her.

Children who are adopted when they are older have sustained many injuries and have usually had a lifetime of rejection. These children are often difficult to love because of all the emotional scars that are a part of them.

There are some advantages to adopting children who are older, however; they will fit into their new family's existing lifestyle better than an infant will and may be more compatible with the children of the couples' friends who got started having children six to ten years earlier.

Still, the disadvantages are many. They spend a lot of time testing the love, the limits, the rules, the privileges, and the patience of those who have promised to take them in and treat them as their very own.

These children usually feel partly to blame for their past. They have probably concluded long ago that the reason their families gave them up and foster parents moved them around a lot was because they were unloveable and/or bad. Children go to great lengths to live up to the labels they believe about themselves.

It takes a great deal of endurance and love for adoptive parents to understand and forgive the child for misbehavior. It is helpful if they try not to expect miracles, don't place blame on the birth parents, reward and reinforce every successive approximation to the goal they have in mind, learn to be consistent, firm, fair, and fun, and refuse to give up.

Usually these children "come around" when they have tested long enough to convince themselves that their new parents are truly "different" and are committed to making this family succeed.

Adoption

For children ages 4 to 8:

Bunin, Catherine and Sherry Bunin. *Is That Your Sister? A True Story of Adoption.* New York: Pantheon Books, 1976. Nonfiction.
    A first-person account of a young girl's feelings about adoption and the process of adoption. The interracial family presents some special situations.

Miles, Miska. *Aaron's Door.* Boston: Atlantic Monthly Press, 1977. Fiction.
    Aaron and his younger sister move in with their new adoptive parents. Aaron's feelings of fear, loneliness, and frustration are clearly identified. A powerful ending enables children to identify with Aaron's desires to belong and to be loved.

Pursell, Margaret Sanford. *A Look At Adoption.* Minneapolis: Lerner Publications Co., 1978. Nonfiction.
    A clear reassuring presentation of adoption which answers many confusing questions for the child. An excellent book to encourage discussion with very young children.

Wasson, Valentina P. *The Chosen Baby.* New York: J. B. Lippincott Co., 1967. Fiction.

A classic about adoption that has been recently updated. It is a family story that can begin a discussion about being "chosen."

For children ages 8 to 12:

Fall, Thomas. *Eddie No-Name*. New York: Pantheon Books, 1963. Fiction.

Eddie, a ten-year-old orphan, visits his prospective parents on their farm. Eddie successfully conquers his fears of adoption. His anxieties are convincingly portrayed.

Silman, Roberta. *Somebody Else's Child*. New York: Frederick Warne and Company, Inc., 1976. Fiction.

Peter, an adopted fourth grader, befriends a school-bus driver. The boy and the old man become close friends. Peter gains a better understanding of the bond between parents and their children, a bond that is just as strong for adopted as for other children.

For children ages 12 to 16:

Bradbury, Bianca. *Laurie*. New York: Ives Washburn, Inc., 1965. Fiction.

Seventeen-year-old Laurie Howe begins to question her true identity. She sets out to find her birth parents. The book raises many unanswered questions an adopted child might have.

Krementz, Jill. *How It Feels To Be Adopted*. New York: Alfred A. Knopf, 1982. Nonfiction.

A fascinating study of nineteen adopted children, ages 8 to 16, who reveal their personal accounts of adoption. The dialogue is candid and convincing.

For adults:

Carney, Ann. *No More Here and There: Adopting the Older Child*. Chapel Hill, North Carolina: University of North Carolina Press, 1976. Nonfiction.

Ms. Carner discusses in straight-forward language the special problems that older children are likely to have and presents practical ways of dealing with them.

Childhood
Stress

Plumez, Jacqueline Horner. *Successful Adoption*. New York: Harmony Books, 1982. Nonfiction.

This book offers a comprehensive analysis of adoption and adoption procedures. State-by-state information on adoption and listings of regional adoption centers and foreign adoption agencies are included.

Sorosky, Arthur D.; Baron, Annette; and Pannor, Reuben. *The Adoption Triangle*. New York: Doubleday-Anchor, 1978. Nonfiction.

This is a study, complete with many case histories, of the effects of sealed records on adopted people, birth parents, and adoptive parents, the three sides of what the authors call "the adoption triangle."

Ideally, the child will emerge from adolescence with a strong sense of identity, as well as a sense of independence.

Chapter Eleven

Latchkey Children

More and more children in today's society are being left alone for some portion of the day, either in the afternoons after school or in the mornings before they leave for the bus. Often, these children are left with a great deal of responsibility—the care of other children.

Although some children are quite capable of managing without their parents and indeed even report that they enjoy the time they have to themselves, others are terrified, lonely, and unhappy.

Some are afraid to tell their parents of their fears, not wanting to disappoint them or make them feel bad, knowing that their parents have enough to worry about as it is.

These children are often told to go straight home, lock themselves in the house, not to answer the phone or doorbell, not to turn on the stove or TV, and to do their homework and/or chores.

Children should be able to have some input about the rules they are expected to obey. It is important for parents to open lines of communication with their children concerning their fears and feelings. Often dialogue can uncover much better ways of handling this time which often hangs heavy on the hands of the child.

Childhood
Stress

There are many positive ways families can handle these difficult times which will help children to cope and grow from the responsibilities that are placed on them.

Fears

Eight-year-old Janie had let herself into the house with the key her parents left in a tin can under the porch. She always hated this time of day—when she had to go into the empty house, alone. She often worried that someone was watching her and was afraid that they would see she was by herself and would try to break in after she got inside.

As she unlocked the door, she called for Patrick, their little dachshund. He came right away, wagging his tail and jumping up to greet her. This helped her feel a little better.

"Hey, Patrick. How're you doing? Did you get lonely or scared here all alone? Well, I'm here now. You don't have to worry. You hungry? Let's get something to eat."

Janie put her books down and walked down the hall to the kitchen, peering carefully into the bathroom and bedrooms as she went by. She stamped her feet as she walked, hoping to scare away anybody who might be hiding in the house.

Loudly she called Patrick. "Come on, puppy, in here. Aren't you hungry?" The dog followed her happily.

After giving Patrick some cookies, Janie poured herself some milk and took her snack into the den. She turned on the T.V. and turned the volume up.

Just when she was getting settled, the telephone rang.

She ran to the phone, thinking it would be her mother.

"Hello, is your mother there?" a man's voice queried.

"She's not able to come to the phone right now. Can I take a message?" Janie repeated her well-rehearsed speech.

"No, that's all right. I'll call back later." He hung up.

Janie worried about what she would say if and when the man called back. She settled back in the den, but found that she wasn't hungry anymore. She threw one of her cookies to Patrick.

"I wish Mom would call. I hate being here by myself."

She looked at the clock on the table. Only 2:45—two and a half hours to go until 5:15, when her mother got home.

Patrick suddenly started barking and ran down the hall. Janie thought, "Suppose he heard someone coming—or worse yet, someone moving in the bedroom or bathroom?"

Janie started crying.

Janie is one of an estimated five to ten million "latchkey children"— children who let themselves into the house and remain there without adult supervision for some part of the day while one or both of their parents are at work. Some of these children are also alone in the mornings before school. Because of increased divorce rates, family mobility, and the changing economy, their number is increasing. Families often feel guilty or frightened about letting their children stay alone; therefore they are reticent to tell others about such arrangements.

The large majority of these children are lonely and scared. They have recurring nightmares as well as many fears: noises, the dark, fire, intruders. Simple noises that are usually ignored—such as tree branches brushing up against a window—send a child's mind racing and can easily become a ghost in the closet.

These are not neglected children. Many of them come from middle income families, often single-parent homes or homes where both parents must work to make ends meet. Because of the soaring cost of daycare and the lack of after-school programs, many working parents feel that their only option is to leave their children alone for part of the day. For the most part, parents outline rules and regulations and teach their children what to do in case of emergencies. But most continue to feel guilty, worry a lot, and hope for the best.

Childhood
Stress

153

Statistics show, in fact, that these children *are* more vulnerable to accidents, injuries, and assaults. There is a higher percentage of child abuse and neglect, sexual molestation, accidents, vandalism, and crime reported among children who are left unsupervised than occurs while an adult is in charge.

Although experts would agree that after–school programs and supervision from adults are better options for children, we nevertheless must face the fact that this is not always possible, and many children will, in fact, be left alone—for part of the day, at least—to fend for themselves.

Temptations and Responsibilities

Benjamin, 6, got off the school bus with his friends, Neil and Todd.

"Come on over and play with us instead of going home," his friends tried to persuade him. "Your dad won't know. You can call from our house."

Benjamin was tempted. He hated to go home alone. But he knew his father expected to hear from him, and he hated to lie to him.

"No, I'd better go home. I'll ask him if I can come over to your house when I call him. Maybe he'll let me. I'll call you."

They parted at his driveway.

Using the key around his neck, Benjamin let himself into the house. He went straight to the phone and called his father's work number. The lady answering said that his dad had stepped out. He would call when he got back.

"Heck," thought Benjamin, "Now I'll have to wait. I wish I had gone over to Neil's. But then he couldn't call me back. I guess it's a good thing I didn't. But I sure wish they could come over here. I don't see why he has so many stupid rules: no company, no fun. I know he won't let me go out. It's no use asking him. He'll just get mad.

He was looking for something to eat when the phone rang.

"Oh, Benjamin. I'm glad you're home." His father's voice sounded cheerful. "Everything okay? You locked the front door, didn't you? Did you find something to eat? I think there's some peanut butter in the cabinet and crackers in the cupboard, unless you and your sister ate it all yesterday. Don't forget to tell Janine to call as soon as she gets home. Yesterday she forgot."

"Dad" Benjamin broke in. "Can't I please go to Neil and Todd's? They invited me over. They have a new video game and I want to play with them. Please, Dad."

"You know the rule, Benjamin. I just can't let you leave the house. Their mother isn't home, and I don't want you unsupervised in their house. Janine will be a little later than usual. But she should be there by 4:00. I'm sorry, Benjamin. I just can't say 'yes.' "

Benjamin was quiet.

"Are you there? Are you all right?"

"Yeah. I'm here."

"Get something to eat and do your homework. The time will pass before you know it. See you later. I have to go now. Bye, Benjamin."

Just as he hung up the phone, the doorbell rang. Having been told never to answer the door, Benjamin stood still in his tracks. "Please go away," he thought.

The doorbell rang again and again.

"Go away," Benjamin muttered under his breath.

Finally, it stopped ringing.

Benjamin took his books and went in the bathroom. He locked the door and stayed there until he heard his sister let herself in the house—an hour and a half later.

Quickly he opened the bathroom door and greeted her. He didn't want her to know that he was a scaredy cat. She would tease him and tell Dad. Dad had enough to worry about.

Latchkey children are usually bored and often lonely and frightened. A child should never be left alone until the parents determine that he is ready for it, can anticipate situations, discuss possible solutions, and show maturity during short periods of time when given the opportunity to be on his own.

There are things parents can do and teach, however, to make such times safer and easier for the child:

- Teach the child to always keep his key out of sight.
- Leave a spare key with a neighbor.
- Go over the route home with the child and determine the amount of time it should take. Tape his name and emergency telephone number inside his coat or lunchbox.
- Make sure the child always has enough money to make a phone call.
- Teach the child to never talk to strangers or get in their car or go anywhere with them.
- If someone scares him, teach him to run and scream.
- If, when the child gets home, he finds anything amiss—the front door open, for example—instruct him not to go in the house but rather to go to a neighbor and call home. If nobody answers, call the police.
- Once inside the house, the child should lock the door and call a parent or neighbor.
- The child should never tell anyone on the phone or at the door that his parents are not at home, but rather should be taught a phrase such as, "My mom can't come to the phone right now. Can I take a message?" When confronted with the direct question, "Is your mother at home?" most children will readily respond honestly, "No." It is difficult for them to lie.

- Emergency phone numbers should be kept near the phone (parent's, police, emergency number, neighbors).

- Teach the child to always answer the phone—it might be you.

- Be sure that the child can see who is at the door. It might be necessary to install a peephole at the child's eye level.

- Make a list of people the child is allowed to visit and who are allowed in the house.

- Teach the child what to do if there is a fire. Practice the procedure. A child can be taught how to put out a contained fire, but if it isn't a small fire, he should locate the siblings, leave the house and call the fire department from a neighbor's. In heavy smoke, the child should be taught to cover his mouth with a wet cloth and crawl to the door.

- If someone tries to break in, the child should be told to try to get out. If that is not possible, he should quietly call the police, go to his room, and lock himself in.

- Teach your child to always leave a note saying where he is going.

- Consider getting a pet. Even a small animal can be company for a child. If the neighborhood is unsafe, a big dog will give him security and status.

- Arrange activities for the child. If at all possible, schedule scouts, library, dancing, or gymnastics on some of the afternoons. Perhaps other parents could take turns carpooling.

- If the child has to be home, give him something to do. Leave him messages on notes or tapes: "When you have set the table (swept the floor, or dusted the den) then you may play with the games or puzzles I left on the shelf in the living room." Take the time to be creative and to leave surprises. Suggest different activities and alternatives to television. Give him something to look forward to.

- Teach him what to do in case of every emergency. Take time to practice drills. Teach safety skills: first aid, relaying information on the phone, dialing emergency numbers (9-1-1).

- Be sure *each* child in the family knows what to do. Don't rely on the oldest to take charge. He may not be home or may panic or be hurt. All children should know how to take care of themselves if the need arises.

- Be sure that you live up to your promises. Call if your child is expecting to hear from you. Arrive home on time. A fifteen-minute stop at the grocery can completely unnerve a child. His imagination can run wild, and he can be sure that you have been killed on the way home.

- Practice problem-solving. Discuss alternatives to situations and see how many ideas and solutions your child can think up:

> What would you do if someone called you names on the bus?
>
> What would you do if someone started bullying or chasing you on your way home?
>
> What would you do if you forgot your key?
>
> What would you do if someone called and asked where your father works?
>
> What if someone called and asked what you were doing?
>
> What would you do if you smelled smoke?
>
> What would you do if the toilet stopped up?
>
> What would you do if you got sick or scared?

Help your children to learn that there is more than one solution to every problem.

Although many children admit to being frightened and lonely when left alone, there are others who report that they enjoy the freedom and responsibility which has been entrusted to them. The long-term effects will be determined by the age and personality of the child as well as his ability to cope with the situations in which he finds himself.

Trying to get caught up at work so she could leave early enough to stop by the store on the way home, Anita was rushing. She received a phone call and when she picked up the receiver, she heard her children on the other end arguing with each other.

"I told you not to call her. She'll be mad."

"I'm going to tell. She told you not to make popcorn, and I'm afraid the house is going to catch on fire."

"Susan, Bernie, what is this? Why are you calling me *again*? I told you not to call me anymore today. My boss is going to get mad at me. I have a lot of work to finish up and I need to stop by the grocery store on my way home. What is it this time?"

"Bernie is making popcorn, and I'm afraid that he is going to start a fire. You told us not to make popcorn, didn't you?" Susan reported.

"Let me talk to Bernie."

After a long pause, Bernie came to the phone. "I'm being careful. I know how to make popcorn. I've done it lots of times before and I've never started a fire. Susan is a scaredy cat. She won't leave me alone. I was talking on the phone to Bill and she got on the other phone and kept giggling and talking. I was so embarrassed. Also, she ate all the cookies. Will you make her behave?"

"Now look you two. Don't call me again. I'm going to lose my job if you keep calling me. Just try to be nice to each other. And, Bernie, be careful with the popcorn. Don't leave the kitchen with it plugged in. Do you hear?"

"What time will you be home, Mom?" "Will it be before dark?"

"As soon as I can—I'll make it by dark if you don't keep calling me."

Anita hung up frustrated.

Children of all ages need independence training, so it is good to start when they are young.

Getting along with brothers and sisters does not happen easily or without effort. Parents need to teach and train their children to cooperate, to work together, to make compromises and to figure out things on their own.

As long as Anita is as nearby as the telephone and will settle their differences for them, Bernie and Susan will continue to call her at work. She needs to be more firm, set unquestionable limits and consequences of misbehavior, and reward and reinforce their positive efforts. She could leave a tape recorder or notebooks for them to record their gripes but promise an extended bedtime or snack if they worked out their differences on their own.

Getting Into Trouble

Phillip, 13, was left home alone every afternoon while his mother was at work. She usually called at 4:00 to check on him. This particular afternoon, she got so busy at work, however, that she forgot to call. At 4:30, the police called her office and asked if she had a child named Phillip.

Of course, she panicked as she said yes. The officer told her that her son had been in an accident and to come right away to the hospital. Unbelieving, she called home—just to made sure—and got no answer.

Beside herself, she drove to the hospital, trying to rationalize that it had to be a mistake. How could he have been involved in an accident? He was supposed to have ridden the school bus home, and she had their only car with her.

When she got to the hospital, she found Phillip in the emergency room along with several of the other neighborhood children and their parents. She was told the story in snatches.

The fourteen-year-old down the street had decided to take the family car around the block and had invited several of the younger children to come along. He lost control of the car as he turned a corner and hit a tree. All the children suffered multiple injuries, but none was seriously injured.

Phillip's mother was relieved and furious at the same time. She didn't know whether to be happy or mad.

No age is the magic age when it is safe or wise for a child to be left alone. Each child should be judged according to his level of maturity, the length of time he will be alone, and his ability to make reasonable decisions. Can the child be counted on to be where he says he will be? Is he on time? Does he follow through on assignments (i.e., chores) when they are given? Does he exercise good judgment when unexpected things happen?

It is hard on children in their early teens to be told that they cannot go outside or play with friends. They hate to feel "different."

At first, children ought to be left only for short periods of time and then an assessment made before longer periods are considered. Leave a routine for a child, including chores for him to do. This gives him a feeling of importance.

Don't scare the child but be realistic about possible dangers—what to do, for example, if a friend asks you to do something you know is dangerous.

Encourage dialogue with your child. Try to find out what he has been doing, how he feels about being left alone, what scares him, what he does when he is lonely or bored. Allow him to express fear, anxiety, boredom. Don't make him feel silly or babyish for feeling the way he does.

Later in life, in retrospect, many adults remember having been left alone with fear and sadness, but they never told anyone. Probably dialogue was not encouraged, and the child concluded that the parent(s) would have been ashamed or disappointed if they knew the truth.

Many parents feel that they have no choice but to leave a child unsupervised for part of the day. It seems to work best when there are clear expectations and routines, close supervision, strong, affectionate family ties and supportive, friendly neighbors.

In an unsupportive environment, there is a higher degree of delinquency, accidents, nightmares, exploitation, sexual abuse, and violence.

The problem of unattended children in our society should be a top concern of communities. There are solutions: more comprehensive child care, kids' survival skills classes, corporate on-site care, centers jointly sponsored by business firms, work adaptations such as flex–time, extended after-school care, and community recreational programs.

It is time to make sure that someone is minding America's children.

Latchkey Children

For children ages 4 to 8:
Blaine, Margery Kay. *The Terrible Thing That Happened at Our House.* New York: Parent's Magazine Press, 1975. Fiction.
   A young girl humorously describes the changes at her house when her mother returns to work.

Iwasaki, Chihiro. *Staying Home Alone on a Rainy Day.* New York: McGraw-Hill Book Co., 1969. Fiction.
   This story describes the loneliness and apprehension a girl feels while her mother is gone.

Sonneborn, R. *Lollipop Party.* New York: Viking Press, 1967. Fiction.
   This book sensitively touches on the feelings of a little boy who waits alone for his mother to come home.

Watson, Pauline. *Days with Daddy.* Englewood Cliffs, NJ: Prentice-Hall, Inc., 1977. Fiction.
   A young boy describes a day with his "house husband" father in this humorous narrative.

For children ages 8 to 12:

Love, Sandra. *But What About Me?* New York: Harcourt Brace,
Jovanovich, 1976. Fiction.

A little girl learns that her mother's job need not undermine
her own sense of well-being and that being more independent
can be fun.

Sawyer, Paul. *Mom's New Job*. Milwaukee, Wis.: Raintree Publishers,
Ltd., 1978. Fiction.

A young girl, whose parents both work, gains new
confidence when she realizes she can take care of herself.

For adults:

Long, Lynette. *On My Own*. Washington, D.C.: Acropolis Books,
1984. Nonfiction.

This book teaches children how to handle emergencies and
daily living. It shows how to make staying alone a positive
experience.

Long, Lynette and Thomas Long. *The Handbook for Latchkey Children
and Their Parents*. New York: Arbor House Publishing Co.,
1983. Nonfiction.

A comprehensive manual which covers a wide variety of
topics. Concrete advice is offered on dealing with minor and
major crises.

*Children of all ages need independence
training, so it is good to start when they are
young.*

Parents need to be aware of problems which often occur when families are separated. Young children often think their father or mother chose to go away, and may blame themselves.

Chapter Twelve

Divorce and Single Parenting

Divorce can represent a major upheaval in the life of a child who has been raised in a two-parent family. There is a great deal of confusion, anger, sadness, fear, and anxiety which the child must face.

If the child is not given sufficient help, the effects will be incorporated within his personality, attitudes, self concept, expectations and eventual world view.

The young child will show his anxiety through regressive behavior, often taking on the apparent symptoms of the adult who is in charge. He may cling, become possessive, tearful, unhappy, unable to sleep or eat.

The preschool child may blame himself and try desperately to bring the absent parent home. He may go to great lengths to contrive reasons for the reunion of the parents and often fantasizes that his parents are still living together.

The school-aged child often takes on the role of the "other" parent. Sometimes he develops "too good" behavior, trying desperately to take care of the custodial parent and make things so desirable that the absent parent will want to come back. He may be unable to concentrate on his schoolwork and lose interest in friends and outside activities.

The adolescent will show more obvious signs of disruption. He usually displays aggressive behavior and takes out his rage on the parent who is most available. Even adults whose parents divorce in later life experience difficult emotions.

All children who suffer from divorce need understanding, help, patience, and "significant others" to help them through the stages that accompany loss. Only then will they finally accept that over which they have no control.

Explanations

Claudia's parents had recently been divorced. Janet had asked her husband to leave because of his uncontrolled temper and said he could come back when he could promise that he would no longer become violent with her and the children. She had begged him to seek counseling, hoping that living without them would bring him to his senses.

However, it hadn't worked out that way. Instead, he was enjoying the best of both worlds. He had moved in with his parents but would come back on weekends and holidays with his back pack and sleep in the den. Each time he returned, Janet, Claudia, 7, and John, 4, hoped that it would be for good. They worked hard to have everything "just right" for him. They fixed his favorite meals, cleaned the house, washed the car, and were careful not to cross him.

One weekend, Tom was visiting and Janet had sent Claudia to clean her room. She had told her not to come out until the room was "decent." Becoming distracted with records and books, Claudia lost track of time. Tom came to check on her and became angry when he saw that she hadn't made any progress.

"You don't care whether I'm here or not. You had a chance to spend time with me and you'd rather listen to records and read. I guess that tells me how important I am. Well, since you don't care about me, I'm leaving. Bye."

Slamming her door, he gathered his belongings and left the house.

Claudia ran to Janet and together they watched him pull out of the driveway. The child was hysterical. Throwing herself on the sofa, she sobbed and sobbed. Janet tried to console her.

"Daddy wasn't really mad at you. We had had another argument, and he was angry with me. Don't blame yourself. He shouldn't have taken it out on you. It's not your fault."

"It *was* my fault. It's all my fault. If it wasn't for me, he would come back here to live. I know it."

There was no convincing her. Claudia cried until she fell asleep on the sofa.

Research tells us that, although children hate the arguments, marital conflict, and physical violence they are exposed to in the home, they have a way of accepting whatever life doles out to them as normal and natural. They assume that other families are like theirs. If a child is abused or mistreated, he concludes that he deserves it and that other children receive similar treatment. If parents argue and fight, the children accept it as being normal. Less than ten percent of all children are actually relieved when the decision for divorce is finally made. It usually throws them into a tailspin no matter how bad the preceding conditions had been.

Statistics show that eighty percent of children are in no way prepared for divorce. They are shocked, pained, and unbelieving when it happens. Then follow the stages of depression, denial, low self-esteem, and guilt.

Young children are usually overwhelmed with feelings of abandonment. They seem obsessed with "Who will take care of me?" "Are you going to leave me too?" "Who will feed me?" and "Who will love me?"

Older children suddenly find the world less reliable and more unpredictable. They worry about not having enough money for clothes and food. They become indifferent and unconcerned about matters that used to seem important.

Children of all ages tend to become sad, moody, and irritable, often tearful, depressed, restless, and frequently physically ill. Some become abnormally obsessed with their parents' physical and mental health.

Children often blame themselves for separation and divorce. Almost all of them want reconciliation at any cost. They dream and fantasize of they day when they will be a family again. Some get sick, devise schemes, try to be "good" enough, or save their lunch money to buy back the missing parent. Children continue to hang on to the hope that their parents will get back together. If one parent abandons the child or even fails to live up to his promises, the child's self-esteem is damaged and he begins to feel that he is unlovable. It is especially difficult when the parent remarries and/or moves away.

Statistics tell us that five years after the divorce, one-fourth of the children have bounced back to their previous productivity and self-esteem, one-half are still muddling through, and one-fourth are deeply troubled—depressed and longing for a return to the pre-divorce times.

Adjusting

Max's grades had been dropping and Ellen was worried about him. She had tried talking to him and to his teacher to see if there was any way she could help. The teacher said that he was not concentrating on his work but that he was capable of doing better.

His mom decided to try a reward system. She knew that Max, 14, wanted a stereo for his room, but she didn't feel that she could afford to give him one. After talking with him about it, she set up a program of rewards.

For every half hour of studying, he could receive a point. For every 5 points, he could get a new tape for his tapedeck, and when he had 50 points, she would buy him the stereo.

At first, Max seemed enthusiastic. He earned several points, straight in a row, but then his interest dwindled. In two weeks, he had only earned 4 points.

Ellen had another talk with him. He promised to do better.

He earned a few more points in the next month, but then he stopped trying altogether.

When he brought his report card home, it was full of failing marks.

That night, Max came to his mother's room and said that he wanted to talk to her. He said that he knew how important his grades were to her, and he felt bad for letting her down. However the reason he hadn't wanted to work to bring his grades up was because he hoped that if his marks were bad enough, his parents would forget how angry they were with each other (they were getting a divorce), and just get mad at him.

He had finally realized that his little plan had not worked.

Children differ in the ways they show stress. Some are angels at home, oversolicitious and helpful. They become mother's right arm.

The job of the home and the school is to help the child reach his highest potential, but we must realize that his potential becomes somewhat limited, temporarily at least, when he is forced to deal with the stressful reality of divorce in his life. In the long run, his ability to cope and adjust will depend on the careful handling and coping mechanisms of those around him.

Playing One Parent Against Another

Gretchen, 5, was spending the weekend with her father. They had done many fun things together, and he was putting her to bed. When she said her prayers, Gretchen asked God to "please make my daddy come back to live with me and Mommy."

When she was climbing in bed, Robert said that he would take her to Disney World if her mother would go along. Gretchen was ecstatic and wanted to get out of bed and call her mother to tell her. Robert told her that the was sure Mommy wasn't home, and she could tell her tomorrow. Gretchen was so excited that she could hardly go to sleep.

The next day when she went home, she ran in the door, calling, "Mommy, Mommy, guess what? Daddy says that he will take us to Disney World. You'll go, won't you, Mommy? Won't you, Mommy?"

Laura came slowly down the stairs, glaring at her ex-husband. To her persistent daughter, she said, "I don't think so, Gretchen. Daddy can take you, but I don't think I'll be able to go with you."

Disappointed, Gretchen looked up at her father, expecting him to say that he would take her. He was angry.

"Well, Gretchen," he said, "there goes our trip. Thanks to your mother, we won't be going to Disney World." With that, he left, slamming the door behind him.

Gretchen was very upset. She flung herself down on the floor and sobbed. Laura tried to comfort her, but she shook her mother's hand away. "You're mean. It's all your fault. Daddy promised me that we would go, and now we can't, all because of you. Don't touch me."

Laura was confused and angry. She had looked forward to Gretchen's return, and now she had an angry and hurt little girl on her hands.

Robert was trying to use Gretchen to get Laura to go on a trip with him. This was an unfair spot in which to put the child. He should never have suggested the trip until he checked it out with her mother. He probably had a pretty good idea that she would not consent to it anyway. He made her look like the villain. She had every reason to be angry with him.

One of the worst things divorced couples can do is to take their frustrations and hurts out on the child. It was cruel to build up her hopes and then to let her down.

Divorce is hard on everyone concerned. Parents who have decided to correct one mistake need to be careful not to make another one by engaging the child in the problem. As long as either or both parties are acting out their hurt, they are likely to further injure the child. Many couples use the child as a pawn. Some will not even talk directly to each other. They talk through the child. ("Tell your mother to buy you some new pajamas." "Tell your father I am waiting for his check.")

If there are children involved, parents owe it to them to behave as adults themselves, to get rid of their hurt as quickly as possible (with counseling, if necessary), and to settle their differences in a mature manner.

As long as they are behaving like children, their children will model their immature behavior and will continue to be affected in many negative ways. They are likely to have trouble growing, sleeping, eating, concentrating, behaving, and learning until their parents are able to get on with their lives, making peace with the past and dealing with the present and future in a productive and healthy way.

There are ways that parents can help to alleviate the suffering of the child and help him recover from this trauma with a minimum number of scars and a reconstructed self-esteem.

First and foremost, the parents need to get their own act together, seeking help when needed. If they remain bitter, vindictive, spiteful, or irresponsible, it will be even harder on the child. If they use him as a pawn or an instrument for hurt, he will suffer more than they. If they continue to act immaturely when they see each other, refusing to treat the former spouse with dignity and respect, the child will be more torn each time there is an encounter.

There are other ways they can help.

- Parents need to explain the divorce to the child. They need to, as much as they can, tell him why they are splitting up and make sure that he knows that he did not cause it and there is nothing he can do to correct it.

- Encourage the child to express he feelings—all of them. It is much better for him to talk about his hurt and anger than to act it out and keep it inside.

- Reassure the child that he will not be "divorced" from the remaining parent. Make sure he knows that he will still be cared for and loved as much as before.

- Help the child to know that his feelings are natural and that, even though things are hard now, time will help heal the hurt, and there will be good times again.

- Provide the child with substitutes, other people with whom he can relate and whom he can learn to trust. Uncles, grandparents, and friends can help a lot.

- Don't let the child take the place of the divorced parent. It is too much burden for him to feel that he has to take Daddy's or Mommy's place, to protect, to comfort, to take care of, or to keep company.

- Help the child to grow up. Encourage his independence and competence. Make him proud of himself.

- Inform the child's teacher. Have a conference and explain to her what has happened. Keep the lines of communication open with the school. Expect some backsliding.

- Let the child know where the money is coming from. If not, he may worry unnecessarily that you will have to sell the house, car, clothes, and belongings. Children have active imaginations and many ungrounded fears. They can deal with reality but not with uncertainties.

- Don't hesitate to seek help for the child, as well as for yourself. There are many people willing and trained to help. Look for them. Ask around. If you feel that you are not getting the help you need, don't hesitate to look elsewhere. Search for a personality match.

- Do not cut the child off from the divorced parent. Encourage the one who moved out to keep in touch with the child. The more involvement the child can count on, the better off he will be. Only forty-five percent of children of divorce have regular contact with both parents. No wonder so many of them are in trouble! A child needs to know that both of his parents still care about him. Don't let your hurt, anger, and disappointment destroy the relationship of the child with his other parent.

- In every way possible, let the child know that he is important to both of you. If you are the absentee parent, call the child every Wednesday, send him a card once a week, see him as often as possible, give him your phone number, maintain an active interest in his life.

Hopefully your child will be one of those who comes out of this experience with flying colors, having acquired some new coping strategies which he can use the next time life deals him a low blow.

Custody Problems

Judd's parents had recently separated. Since they lived a short distance from each other, they had decided that it would be best for him to spend two days with each parent and then switch off. This would give him alternate weekends with each and would give them equal amounts of freedom. The marriage counselor had suggested this arrangement, and they had agreed that it would be best for all concerned.

When Jeff and Cathy had confronted Judd, 9, with their decision to separate, he had been quite upset. He screamed and yelled, threw things, and told his mother that it was all her fault. He had told them that they were both stupid and he wasn't going anywhere.

They had accepted his anger and allowed him to express himself freely.

When the time did come to separate, he packed his things and left with his mother.

Two days were up, and it was time for him to ride the school bus to his father's. Instead, he returned to his mother's. When Jeff got home from work and found Judd not there, he called Cathy.

His son answered. "Hey, Judd, why are you at Mom's? You were supposed to come here. You knew that. What happened?"

"I'm not coming there until next week. I decided that I wanted to switch off and spend every other week with each of you. That suits me better. So I'll be there on Saturday."

"Did Mom tell you that would be okay?" Jeff was angry.

"I didn't tell her yet. She's still at work."

"Well, I don't like it. That was not the plan. You know you were supposed to come here, and you should have followed through. I'm coming to get you—now!"

"Oh, no, you're not. I won't come with you. I'm staying here." Judd hung up the phone.

Jeff was in a dilemma. He was mad. It didn't suit him at all for Judd to change the plans. He waited for Cathy to get home and called her.

Not feeling very good about her, the conversation was strained.

"Well, I don't see that it matters that much," she said. "I think you're making a mountain out of a molehill. But then, you always did like to do that. For goodness sake, hasn't he gone through enough? Let him stay. I don't care. It's not worth the hassle." She hung up.

Jeff was angry and felt that he had been had. He was uneasy that a nine-year-old had been allowed to reverse a decision which had been carefully made by three adults. He was afraid that Judd would keep right on making decisions which were not his to make and, in the long run, would gradually begin to feel that he did not have to obey any rules if they did not suit him.

Judd's father had a valid point. A nine-year-old cannot possibly know what is best for him in all situations. He needs the security of knowing that people who are older and wiser and who have his best interests at heart will step in to enforce the rules.

Jeff's hunches are well grounded. Judd will gain strength in the fact that his counter plan worked, and this will give him the incentive to "be the boss." In time, both parents may feel that no matter what they tell him to do, he will obey only if it suits him.

This is not to say that Judd's feelings and opinions should not be considered. Jeff could have said, "Your mother and I will talk with the counselor about this at our next session, but for now, the present plan sticks. I'm coming to get you."

At a time of disruption, such as divorce, parents are more vulnerable. This often causes them to doubt their own judgment and to be easily persuaded to back down.

Especially at such times of uncertainty and disruption, children need a life they can count on, as well as parents who are still able to make wise decisions on their behalf and stick to them.

In the long run, the child will emerge much more secure and stable and able to live with decisions over which he has no control.

> Becky, 12, and Billy, 11, had spent the winter in Florida with their father and stepmother. The children's mother, Sharon, had come to pick them up: they were to attend her wedding, spend a week with their grandmother, and then spend the summer in Virginia with their mother and new stepfather.
>
> When it was time to leave his father's house, Billy was very quiet. Sharon asked him what was wrong, but he wouldn't answer. That night in the motel, he finally confided that the night before she arrived to pick them up, his father had come

home drunk. He told Billy that the reason he had gotten drunk was because Billy and his sister were leaving.

The child felt responsible for his father's drinking and felt guilty for leaving. He was also worried that his father would keep on drinking because he missed him and his sister.

Sharon tried to tell Billy that he was not responsible for his father's behavior and should not blame himself. She was very angry with her former husband for making their son feel guilty.

Many children are uprooted in the summer to spend time with the "other" parent. It is a difficult transition for children and parents alike. Children have a hard enough time dealing with such transitions in their lives without picking up the blame for their parents' weaknesses.

Children who are disrupted from familiar surroundings to go live with a parent and new stepparent have a big adjustment to make. They need all the loving support they can get from all the people who care about them.

It is important that they not be held responsible for any trouble (such as alcoholism) which is present in either family.

Adults Whose Parents Divorce

Jane was 28 when she learned that her parents were planning to get a divorce. Her mom had called and asked if Jane could come home that weekend. When she asked if there was something wrong, her mother said she would tell her the whole story when she got there.

Jane felt uneasy as she drove the 150 miles to her parents' home.

As soon as she saw her mother, she knew that her hunches had been right.

"What is it, Mom? What's wrong? You look awful."

Lois broke down and told her the whole story. Jane's father had been having an affair with his secretary. It must have been going on for several years, but her mom had just learned about it six months ago.

She had been shocked when, out of the clear blue, he had announced one night that he wanted a divorce. Lois cried, begged, bargained, and prodded to find out what was wrong, until he finally told her that he was in love with another woman. At first she had hoped to win him back, but now she knew there was no use. He had moved out and they were going through with their plans to split up.

Jane was devastated. She knew that her mother needed her support and help, but she just felt like she wanted to leave. She couldn't let her Mom know how upset she was.

She left as soon as she could and went back to her own home, hoping that there she would find some relief from her hurt and anger. However, it didn't subside. She felt angry at both her parents for betraying her, but especially at her father for hurting her mother.

Jane vowed never to see or speak to her father again.

When divorce comes to the parents of teenagers and even to adults, it is still traumatic in their lives. Even if they grow up listening to quarrels and harsh words and lay awake hearing their parents fighting, there was always the fear, the unthinkable horror and ultimate dread that the turmoil would end in divorce.

Many parents wait until the last child leaves home, thinking that the separation will be less of a blow at that time. They tend to think that the "almost grown-up" child will take the news maturely, will understand everything, and be able to carry on with his life with no changes. This is simply not so.

A prominent college president asks parents each year at freshman orientation not to get divorced over the next four years because it can severely affect the student's well-being.

Gunhild Hagestad, a Penn State University sociologist, interviewed college students whose parents were divorced within the previous 3 years, and found them to be devastated. They felt as if the bottom had dropped out of their lives.

In order for children to be able to leave home, to make good decisions for themselves, to concentrate on their work and to be relatively secure, they need a strong base back home upon which they can depend and rely. If children feel that their family is collapsing, they have no one to turn to. They don't feel that they can come home to their parents with problems because parents have enough of their own.

Children suddenly faced with the news of their parents' divorce often begin to suffer difficulty. They find their work boring, their relationships unsatisfying, their enthusiasm to plan for the future drained, and their energy sapped.

Anxiety, anger, guilt, and depression often set in. They are late to work, oversleep classes, lose their appetites, overeat, increase their use of alcohol or drugs or become bored with everyone and everything. They worry about their parents on the one hand, but on the other hand, are angry with them for "doing this to them." They become anxious about going back home to a house divided and unfamiliar.

Frequently, parents put added strain on the children and use them as messengers. "Tell your mother to call the insurance people." "Tell your father you need some money." They try to get their children to take sides. The child, caught in the middle, feels used and resentful.

Here are some suggestions to parents of older adolescents and young adults, who have decided that divorce is the only answer for them:

- Keep your child fully informed. Don't spring any surprises.
- Expect the child to be upset, angry, and hurt.
- Try to remain objective and supportive of each family member.
- Make sure that the child doesn't feel responsible.
- Don't put the child in the middle.

- Allow the child to freely express his own feelings. Counseling is free to students on college campuses; encourage him to take advantage of it.

Remember that the ability to cope with stress is learned, and that the way parents handle this crisis will greatly influence the resources the child will find to survive this traumatic experience.

The Single Parent

Jonathan, 4, had been put to bed but refused to stay there. He was still awake when it was time for Diana to go to bed. After the lights were off, she felt a tap on her shoulder and heard a little voice saying, "Mommy, I'm scared. Can I get in bed with you?" Diana, recently divorced, who was tired and a little lonely, too, gave in and let Jonathan get in bed with her.

Jonathan will probably repeat this procedure many times. It will possibly become a habit; one that is very hard to break.

Many children go through a stage of not wanting to sleep alone. It is probably not best to let them sleep in the bed with the parent, for this might only verify the child's fears that it is not really safe to be alone. It would be best for Diana to remind him that he has a bed of his own and so does she. (Parents need and deserve their privacy.) It may be necessary for her to go back to his room with him, rub his back, leave a night light on, or sit with him a few minutes. If she does this consistently, he will learn that she means business.

When one parent moves out of the home, the disruption that results definitely affects all persons involved, children included. Even though this is a difficult time for everyone, there are some precautions we can take to make the transaction less painful.

Children often become fearful that, if one parent walks out, the other parent might do the same. It may take many conversations to fully convince the child.

Many parents have the mistaken notion that they can spare their children the pain which accompanies divorce and separation. Children will certainly be affected and they need help to recognize and deal with the realities. Otherwise, they may withdraw, fantasize, blame themselves, or live with hidden terrors that may affect their behavior and self-concepts the rest of their lives.

The child needs to be assured that even though the parents no longer care for each other, this in no way affects their caring for him. He may need to be told many times and in many ways that both parents still love him and always will (and would never divorce him!).

Parents should make it very clear to the child that he was in no way responsible for the divorce and that he does not have the power to bring the parents back together.

A child should not have to feel the burden of having to take the place of the absent parent ("You'll have to be the man of the house now"). This could become an emotional burden too heavy for any child to bear.

Parents should not involve the child in their feelings of hatred and revenge. They should avoid using him as a pawn, a spy, a weapon, or a witness to "get back" at each other. It isn't fair to drag him into adult battles. A child will suffer the least amount of damage when parents act as mature adults and are careful not to destroy the child's loyalty to both parents.

A child should be given honest, simple answers to his questions. He does not need elaborate details which might be frightening or threatening, but he will be uneasy and insecure if he is not dealt with honestly.

Parents should resist the temptation to overindulge the child because they feel guilty about the divorce. It is much more important to give the child your time rather than lots of new toys. Do not let money and material possessions become substitutes for love.

It is important for both parents to be as consistent as possible in maintaining limits for the child. He needs to feel that they are confident and are still in charge of his world.

Children of divorce should be allowed—even encouraged—to express themselves: their anxieties, hurts, fears, and feelings of loss, rejection, guilt, and anger. They need a sympathetic shoulder to lean on through a confusing and painful time.

As time passes, and as they observe their parents successfully reorganize their own lives, children will see that divorce is not the end of the world—that life does go on—and that a once-collapsing world can result in personal and social readjustment and growth for all of those involved.

> Ethel had just told Carol, 5, to pick up her toys and get ready to go to bed. Carol ignored her mother's request and continued to play with the toys. Ethel became angry and threatened to spank Carol if she didn't stop "right now." Carol kept playing, and Ethel carried through and spanked her.
>
> Carol cried, "You're mean, and that's why Daddy left us. You hollered at him, too. I'm going to live with him. He would be nice to me and wouldn't spank me every night."
>
> Ethel was furious.
>
> "All right. Why don't you call him and tell him to come get you. If he loves you so much, why doesn't he call when he's supposed to? He promised to take you to the zoo last week, didn't he? And he never showed up. Go on and live with him, if you want to. You'll find out who's good to you."
>
> Carol went crying to her room and her mother turned on the television to get her mind off their argument.
>
> When Ethel went up to check on Carol later, she found the child asleep beside a little suitcase which she had packed with a doll, slippers, and a nightgown.

Carol has probably found her mother's "sore spot" and is playing it for all it's worth. Naturally, it hurts and makes her mother mad. It would help if Ethel could tell Carol how she feels. She could tell her that it is all right for her to be angry and to talk about it, but it is not fair for her to take her frustrations out on her. Ethel should try not to react to her verbal insults. Perhaps, she could set aside some time each day to talk with Carol, when she can answer her questions about the divorce and accept her hurts and resentments.

Ethel could tell Carol that every night, right after dinner, they will talk about the divorce for fifteen minutes, but she doesn't want Carol to say mean things to her about it any other time. Even though children need to be able to express themselves, it is sometimes wise to set limits and parameters so that it won't get out of hand.

Marge had a date and had made arrangements for the boys to spend the night with their grandparents. The plans had been discussed thoroughly ahead of time.

Six-year-old Robbie, was quite inquisitive about his mother's date. "What are you going to do? Where are you going? How late will you be out? What does he look like? Are you going to keep this one?"

Marge had answered all his questions patiently.

When it came time to go to the grandparents, Robbie became obstinate. "I'm not going. I'm going to stay home."

"No, Robbie, you are going." She practically had to drag him to the car. All the way, he protested. "I'm not going to let you ruin my evening," Marge said. "Your grandparents are expecting you. It wouldn't be fair to disappoint them now."

When they arrived at the grandparents, Robbie stood his ground. He refused to get out of the car.

Marge was desperate. "Please, Robbie. I am losing patience with you. Come on." She stood outside the car and begged.

Nothing happened. He didn't budge. She tried to yank him from the car but couldn't.

Marge went in the house and told Grandmother that she

couldn't get Robbie to come in. She guessed that she would have to call off her date. She went back to the car and asked Ricky, 4, if he wanted to stay or come with her. He said he wanted to go home, too.

Marge left with the boys, went home, and called off her date. She was resentful and hardly spoke to Robbie all evening.

Finding yourself suddenly single brings many hassles, even if the separation was your idea and a welcome relief.

For example: you have no one to turn to for support, relief, understanding, help, and protection, no one else to take over when you have a headache, to care when your child is sick, to turn out the lights, or to help when the car won't start.

You have pangs of guilt: where did I fail? What have I done to the children?

You miss adult companionship, someone to talk to (even if it was to argue with), to share the past, and plan for the future.

At times, you resent having the children twenty-four hours a day and seven days a week. This is unsettling since you worked hard to deserve custody.

You feel let down and angry and need to cry a lot and lash out at your "ex," your child, your mother, anybody who's close by.

Just when you think you're making it, a phone call, a familiar song, a television show, or an old photo can throw you, and you become unglued all over again.

It is a help to realize that these feelings are natural and inevitable. There are, however, steps which can be taken to help.

- Try to overcome guilt. Tell yourself that you did the best you could with your marriage and you are going to keep on doing the best you can with your new life-style.

- Take pride in your accomplishments: find out that you can make good decisions, take care of the car, cook, mow the grass, and juggle the checkbook.

- Don't try to be both father and mother. Call on others to substitute instead of trying to do both jobs yourself. Many people would love to be of help. Let them feel the joy which comes from sharing their lives with children.

- Bone up on your parenting skills. Take a course. Read a book. Don't let your children take over and control you.

- Don't try to be a super-parent. Establish rules. Divide the chores. Let the children know how much you need them to pitch in and help. One of the positive outcomes of divorce is more competent, self-sufficient children.

- Don't deprive yourself for your children. They can stand some deprivation and, in the long run, they will be better off if you look out for your own needs. Living the martyr role leads to resentment for you and ingratitude for them. Keep your own personal space and demand some privacy.

- Simplify your life as much as possible. Your time is your most precious possession. Don't waste it. Sacrifice some of your high standards for elaborate meals, a spotless house, nightly bath routines. Look for ways to cut corners. Board a college student who will help with babysitting. Exchange services with neighbors or friends. Organize a baby-sitting co-op.

- Don't feel upset when you are tired of the children. Realize that you have a hard job and that, at times, you are overwhelmed with the responsibility.

- Do everything possible to encourage your former spouse to assume responsibility for the children. Keep your relationship as friendly as possible. Your children will have fewer problems and your burden will definitely be lighter if the job of child–rearing is shared physically, financially, and emotionally. If there is so much anger and hurt that you are immobilized and unable to act civilized toward your children's other parent, seek help.

- Don't compete for being the favorite parent. The absent parent often tries to "buy" the child's love with gifts, trips and favors. Children will eventually see through the superficiality and will be more grateful for quality time spent listening, talking, or playing together.

- Don't criticize your child's other parent. It's all right to state the facts, "Johnny was upset when you didn't call," or "I wish your mother would hurry up," but if you run him/her in the ground, the child often takes it personally, adding to his confusion and turmoil.

- When your children are with your former spouse, don't sit home and be lonely. Plan something you would like to enjoy. Shop with a friend, go to a movie, play tennis, change your hairstyle. Indulge yourself. Do something to lift your spirits. This will make you a better parent and a happier person.

- Look out for yourself. Your self-concept is paramount to the way your children will feel about themselves. Make a list of the things you have always wanted to do: go back to school, lose weight, take an exercise class, piano lessons, needlepoint, dancing lessons, or business course.

- Realize that life must go on, and although none of us would choose the bumps in the road, sometimes they make us wiser, stronger and more fulfilled people.

Patrick, 9, and Brad, 13, were visiting their father for the weekend. He had a date on Saturday evening and had made arrangements for the boys to stay with their grandmother. However, he had not told the boys about it until he was ready to take them to her house.

When he heard that his father was going out, Patrick was very upset. All the way to his grandmother's house, he whined and cried. Dirk, in exasperation, slapped him. Patrick got very quiet and then his father felt guilty. When they got to their grandmother's, he tried to talk to Patrick, but Patrick wouldn't listen. Dirk, feeling very confused, told his son that he could go with him on his date.

Since Dirk knew of his date before the weekend, he could have prepared Patrick ahead of time for the fact that he was going to stay at his grandmother's. We often put off telling our children something unpleasant because we dread their reactions. However, even though it is not always easy, it is more fair to give advance notice and let the child have time to adjust to unpleasant news and reconcile himself to having to do something he doesn't want to do. All of us respond better when we know ahead of time what is expected of us, rather than having surprises sprung on us.

Dirk's dad fell into the same trap many other parents experience quite frequently:

- They tell the child to do something.
- The child complains with whining, crying, pouting, or sulking.
- The parent reacts negatively, often punitively.
- The child becomes sullen.
- The parent feels guilty and reverses his original decision, often against his better judgment.

When this happens, the child has learned that his whining and crying pay off, and he will try this procedure again when he is told to do something he doesn't want to.

Parents need to learn some new skills in handling sticky situations like the one mentioned above. Obviously, slapping Patrick did nothing to improve the situation. In fact, it probably made it worse: the child was angrier and the father felt guiltier.

If Dirk did not tell Patrick ahead of time about the change of plans, it probably would have been a good idea for him to explain the situation to Patrick, accept the child's disappointment, express his regret for the conflict, and then go on with his plans. He might have worked out an arrangement or a compromise with Patrick. "Since I can't be with you tonight, I'll come to Grandmother's in the morning and we'll cook your favorite breakfast," or "If you will be pleasant at Grandmother's tonight, you and I can go fishing in the afternoon," or "get a pizza on the way home tomorrow."

Although we want to allow plenty of room for children to be able to express their feelings, we have to be careful not to go against our better judgment and change our plans as a result of their inappropriate behavior and reactions. This gives them too much power and causes parents to become justifiably resentful and bitter. As a result, then, they find it difficult to be as loving and caring as their children need them to be.

> Casey's parents had been divorced since he was a year old. Since his friends at kindergarten had never met Casey's father, the child asked Randy if he would take off work to go with him to the class picnic. Marie promised to make brownies for them to take. Casey, 4, bragged to all his friends that his dad was coming to the picnic. He was so excited the night before that he had trouble going to sleep. "I can't wait for my friends to meet Daddy," he told Marie.
>
> Late that night, after Casey was asleep, the phone rang. "Marie, this is Randy. I can't take Casey to the picnic in the morning."
>
> "You've got to be kidding. Do you know how much he is counting on it? He's been bragging to his friends at school all week, telling them that his dad was going to take off work for the picnic. And you wait until you knew he was asleep to call so I would have to be the one to tell him. What's your excuse this time?"
>
> "Well, you won't like it, but I'm going to play golf. These friends of mine came into the store tonight and asked me to go with them. I just couldn't turn them down."
>
> "And what do you want me to tell Casey? You know he'll be heartbroken."
>
> "Tell him anything you want. I'll call him tomorrow night."

Marie slammed down the phone. "Typical," she thought. "How did I ever stay married to that man?"

The next morning when she told Casey that Randy wasn't going to take him to the picnic, the child's face fell. "But who will go? You have to go to work, don't you?"

Marie felt so sorry for Casey that she took the day off from work, without pay, to go with him.

This is one of the saddest things that can happen to a child. Every child needs to think well of his parents even when the parents do not think well of each other. It is best for parents not to run each other down in front of the child. I think that the only thing for the mother to do in a case like this is to help the child cope with his own feelings. "I know you must be hurt. I'm sorry your daddy let you down. I wish he wouldn't do this to you." The child knows whom he can count on. There is no need to remind him. He is hurt enough already.

If the mother has any power left with the father, it would be wise to write or talk with him and tell him how upset this kind of behavior makes his son. She could ask him to please be more careful in the future not to promise anything he cannot deliver. Beyond this, there is nothing else she can do except to help her son with his own disappointments and hurts. This takes a very special way of handling.

Stuart's parents had been divorced for a year. They had informal joint custody arrangements, where Dad picked his four-year-old son up from school on certain days, kept him part of the week and the week-ends were split between the two homes.

Ginger called her former husband's office to remind him that today was his day to pick up Stuart. He was out of the office, so she left a message for him to return her call. At 2:30, she tried his office again and found that he had not returned.

Afraid that he had forgotten, she left work and rushed to school to check on her son. Sure enough, Stuart was waiting.

"C'mon, Stuart, hop in. I don't know where your father is. He has probably forgotten that he was to pick you up. I'll take you to his house. I'm sure the sitter is there."

"But I wanted Daddy. He promised that we could stop for ice cream on the way home today. Where is he? Maybe he is coming. Can't I wait for him?"

"No, heaven knows where he is. I'm afraid to leave you here. I'll stop and get you some ice cream. Just hurry up. I'm supposed to be at work."

Ginger was frustrated and hassled. She hurried to the ice cream store.

"Daddy said he was going to take me to the movies tonight. I hope he hasn't forgotten that, too," Stuart told his mother, while licking his cone.

"Well, I hope he remembers. I wouldn't count on it though."

When she got to her former husband's house, she hurried Stuart up to the door. She rang the bell and waited impatiently.

When the sitter came to the door, Ginger demanded, "Do you know where Rodney is? He was supposed to pick up Stuart. Did he say when he would be home?"

"He is on the phone now. Do you want to speak with him?"

Ginger went in the house and picked up the receiver. "Where are you? You knew this was your day to pick him up. I left work to get him and that's not fair. Are you going to take him to the movies? He is counting on it. You promised. Why should I be the one to tell him? Okay, but I think that's mean—to promise and then back down. Why can't you? Oh, forget it!" Ginger slammed down the phone.

Stuart was watching her. "What did he say? Is he coming to take me to the movies?"

"No, he isn't. I'm sorry. Maybe I can come back later and take you out. I'll call when I get off work. I'm sorry. You know how Daddy is."

Ginger came back after work and took Stuart to the movies. Then she took him home with her.

Ginger is assuming the responsibility for Rod's custody. As long as she will pick up the slack, he will let her do it.

Sooner or later, Stuart will have to come to grips with the strengths and weaknesses of both his parents. Ginger cannot shield him forever from the realities.

Rod is accustomed to having his former wife assume most of the responsibility for their son. Even though he says he wants joint custody, he frequently "forgets" to hold up his end of the bargain. As long as she calls to remind him and picks up the pieces when he falls down, he will let her do it.

Actually, she is preventing her son and his father from coming to terms with each other. Until she decides to stop, her "ex" will probably remain irresponsible and helpless.

It would be wise for Ginger to decide to let go of the relationship between Stuart and Rod. She could tell Stuart's father that from now on, she is getting out of it. When they make arrangements, she will expect him to remember. If he disappoints his son, it is up to him to work it out between them. She should encourage Stuart to speak up for himself and to tell Rod how he feels when he forgets to pick him up or breaks his promises.

If he continues to fall down, renegotiations concerning the joint custody arrangements should be made between the two adults.

Ginger is running herself ragged, building up resentment, and accomplishing nothing by doing for someone else what he should be doing for himself. When she decides to stop, he will be forced to decide whether to lose the relationship with his son or to grow up and become a responsible adult and parent.

Benjamin's mother had never been married. He had never known a father and had never asked Terri about it. The conversation had never come up, so she assumed that he had never wondered. She hoped that he would never ask, because she didn't know how she could ever explain the situation to him.

Terri had trouble when people asked her about Benjamin's father, but she had learned to answer calmly. "I'm not married."

Terry was washing dishes watching out the window where Benjamin was playing with two of his little friends. She could hear them talking.

"Benjamin, where is your daddy?" asked one of the little boys.

"I don't have a daddy," was his quick reply.

"My mother says that everybody has a daddy," another little friend chimed in.

"Well I don't," said Benjamin quietly.

Terri was thankful that the subject was not pursued any further, but she worried about what might be said next time.

Every child will eventually come to realize that he has both a father and a mother. If it is never discussed with him, he will assume that it is a subject that should not be mentioned. Then he will fantasize or make up a "dream" father. He might devise a story that is very far-fetched, but he will come to believe it. This is dangerous, for he could blame himself or blame his mother that the relationship didn't work out.

It would be better to tell him something that is true. Terri could tell him that she and his father loved each other at one time, but she was too young to become a wife, or he wasn't ready to get married, or he needed to go on with school or they stopped loving each other. At any rate, they realized that they could not make a life together, so they did not get married. It would be good to let him know that his father was very special to Terri at one time, even though they agreed later to go separate ways. She could tell him some good things about his father, so that as he grows up, he will know that part of him is not "all bad." Children are better off with information, even if it is sad, than no information at all.

Divorce and Single Parenting

For children ages 4 to 8:

Goff, Beth. *Where is Daddy? The Story of a Divorce*. Boston: Beacon Press, 1969. Fiction.

> An unflinching portrayal of the anger of divorce. Grief, confusion, and loneliness of a four-year-old girl are touchingly portrayed.

Lisker, Sonia Olson and Leigh Dean. *Two Special Cards*. New York: Harcourt Brace Jovanovich, Inc., 1976. Fiction.

> Saddened by her parents' divorce, a little girl finds she can love each parent individually and that both still love her.

Pursell, Margaret Sanford. *A Look at Divorce*. Lerner Publications Co., 1976. Nonfiction.

> This short book views divorce as a solution to unhappiness, leading in most cases to happiness.

For children ages 8 to 12:

Berger, Terry. *How Does It Feel When Your Parents Get A Divorce*? New York: Julian Messner, 1977. Nonfiction.

> This book discusses problems and emotions young people experience when parents divorce, the family separates, and life-styles change.

Blume, Judy. *It's Not the End of the World*. Scarsdale, NY: Bradbury Press, Inc., 1972. Fiction.

This book describes a divorce seen through the eyes of three children. The feelings and behavioral reactions of all three youngsters are portrayed.

Gardner, Richard A. *The Boys and Girls Book About Divorce*. New York: Jason Aronson, Inc., 1970. Nonfiction.
An extremely helpful book for older children to read about divorce.

Lexau, Joan M. *Me Day*. New York: Dial Press Inc., 1971. Fiction.
The book recalls the events leading to the parents' divorce.

For children ages 12 to 16:

Greene, Constance C. *A Girl Called Al*. New York: Viking, 1969. Fiction.
This candid first-person narrative deals with a teenager's image of herself and how she overcomes her feelings of loneliness and rejection.

Le Shan, Eda J. *What's Going to Happen to Me*? New York: Four Winds Press, 1978. Nonfiction.
This book helps children understand themselves and their parents better and accept their situation without guilt, fear, or other disturbing emotions.

For adults:

Despert, J. Louise. *Children of Divorce*. New York: Doubleday, 1953. Nonfiction.
This book focuses on parents confronting the problem of their child's emotional adjustment during the process of divorce and afterward.

Grollman, Earl. *Talking About Divorce: A Dialogue Between Parent and Child*. Boston: Beacon Press, 1975. Nonfiction.
A helpful book for divorced parents in explaining divorce to the children involved and helping them to accept it.

Over a half million adults in the United States take on a new role every year, that of "parent-by-marriage."

Chapter Thirteen

Step-life and Blending Families

The normal demands of living in a family require many adjustments, compromises, and disappointments and at times seem impossible to work out.

However, when two families attempt to merge, the problems they face are at times unbelievable and seem insurmountable.

Each person in the new arrangement comes with a "history"—with bad and good memories of the past and bad and good expectations for the future. Each is necessarily in a position to try to protect himself from further hurt. Each is vulnerable and filled with mixed emotions. Although, at times, there is hope that the new arrangement will work, there is ambivilence at best, knowing that if it does, this could mean admitting that there was something wrong in the previous arrangement.

Many times the people who are thrown together in a blended family are not necessarily drawn to each other even as friends, much less as family members. There is bound to be added competition, disagreement, divided loyalties, need for blame, confusion, anger, and hurt.

It takes time, commitment, and patience on the part of everyone involved to make "step-life" even manageable, to say nothing of being rewarding and pleasant.

To be aware of the potential hazards involved is the first step.

Hazards

Donny, 4, had been playing in the den waiting for dinner. When his stepfather came home from work, he passed by the door without saying anything. The child called out, "Hi, Bill," but there was no answer.

Instead, he went to the kitchen looking for his wife.

"Can't you say 'hi' to Donny?," Liz asked him before he had had a chance to greet her.

Bill chose to ignore the question and asked her what was for supper. She pulled away as he offered a kiss on the cheek.

"Well, that's a fine way to be greeted," he grumbled, as he left the room.

When Liz called her husband and son to dinner, Donny didn't come. Checking on him, she found that he had wet his pants.

Just as Bill sat down to eat, Liz called that she would be there in a minute because she had to change Donny's pants.

Annoyed, Bill came to investigate. "What's wrong with the baby? You're too soft on him. Here, I'll take care of it."

He grabbed Donny and spanked him hard on his bottom. "Now, you go and change your own pants, young man. You're much too old to be having accidents. You hear?"

Upset, Donny ran to his room and slammed the door so hard that the knob hit against the wall and broke the plaster.

Bill followed close behind. "Okay, that does it. You just stay in your room and forget supper."

Liz was angry, feeling that Bill was much too harsh.

That night, worried about Donny, and still mad at her husband, she chose to sleep with her son.

Over a half million adults in the United States take on a new role every year, that of "parent-by-marriage." This means that approximately one million children become stepchildren. The word "stepparent" usually evokes negative feelings, partly because of traditional fairy tales (Hansel and Gretel, Cinderella, and Snow White), and partly because it is, in truth, a difficult role to fill.

The prefix "step" implies "acquired" and "not by choice," and stepchildren are "part of the package deal." Stepparents have the difficult position of entering a family with a history where someone else who was at one time important is no longer present. It is no wonder that this new role is difficult, scary, and complex. Living with one's "inherited" children is even more complicated.

Some of the reasons why stepparenting is difficult are:

- Each parent has his own past history and set way of doing things.

- Each comes to the new family with unrealistically high hopes ("Things will be better this time." "You love me, you'll love my children.")

- Everyone involved has suffered hurt in the past and is trying to protect himself from more hurt.

- The stepmother starts out with a mythical black eye: usually seen as wicked, cruel, and responsible for discipline and punishment. Little, however, is expected of the stepfather (except that he make enough money to support two families).

- Stepparents do not have a chance to choose their stepchildren; they came along with the deal. Without blood ties, there is little chance that they would even like—much less love—each other.

- Natural parents see their own children through rose-colored glasses. They have a mutual investment and therefore need to see the best qualities in their own children. (It feeds their own ego.) Stepparents have no such need. They are more objective and often brutally frank.

- Stepparents have certain expectations of children: they should wash their hands before dinner, be on time, keep their rooms neat, and say "thank you." It is a difficult assignment to raise children that you didn't "start from scratch."

- The stepmother feels a need to prove that she was a better choice than the children's mother. She tries to be a better housekeeper, cook, lovemaker, companion, game player, laundress, and career girl. Besides becoming quickly exhausted, she finds that this is rarely noticed, much less appreciated.

- The children cannot admit the new stepmother's positive traits for two reasons: they are afraid of getting attached to her and then hurt again, and they don't want to be disloyal to their biological parent. (Children wear rose-colored glasses, too.)

- When the stepmother has gone "all out" to provide the perfect environment for her new family and is met with indifference, ingratitude, and hostility, she eventually withdraws. Since this was what the children thought would happen, their predictions came true.

- To make matters more complicated, there are grandparents and in-laws, who are also included in the package deal, encumbered with their own set of hurts, opinions, and suggestions.

- Stepfathers find themselves spending more time with their stepchildren than their own children and may become resentful.

- There are too many people involved in the second marriage. The former spouse seems to be everywhere—in conversations, traditions, memories, and the children's looks and personalities. It is impossible to escape the influence. If the original parent has died, there is a tendency to make him a saint. This is a hard act to follow.

- Money presents an enormous problem to step-families. No one is satisfied. The former wife complains that she never has enough. The new wife feels that she works for the former wife. If the children are older, they may have been opposed to the marriage from the beginning, for fear they would receive less inheritance. Often there is constant bickering and petty arguing even to the extent of some wanting others to be written out of the will.

- The children feel hostile if their biological parent does not take an interest in them. They also feel pushed and pulled when they are sent back and forth from one home to another at the convenience of other people's schedules and social lives. Each re-entry is difficult and requires new adjustments.

- When there are hard feelings between the original couple, the new spouse and children are usually the ones who catch the brunt of the hostility, the grumpiness, the moods and the complaining.

Children have a difficult time adjusting to other children who may be included in the arrangement. They are expected to share bedrooms, space, allowances, and love with step-siblings whom they may not even like.

Stepchildren will test to see who's the boss. If the stepparent tries to discipline, they will run to their own parent for help. Most parents are partial to their own children, and this presents daily problems and adjustments. One parent sides with the child, someone is left out—usually the stepparent—and this takes its toll on the marriage, which is the hub of the wheel and the central force which will determine whether or not this new arrangement will dissolve or survive.

Kitty, 8, was coming to spend the weekend with her father and stepmother as usual. Holly who had only been married for a year, was still trying hard to win her stepdaughter's love and trust. She had worked to make the weekends special, by planning special events and trips to Kitty's favorite places. Some weekends went well. Others didn't.

This week, Holly had wanted to surprise Kitty by making her a new dress. She had spent every night working on it, and it had turned out just as she had wanted. She could hardly wait for Kitty to see it.

When Jim picked his daughter up, he told her that Susan had a surprise for her.

"Where's my surprise?" Kitty greeted her stepmother.

Disappointed that Jim had told her, Holly got the dress and carried it into the room for Kitty to see.

"Oh, is that all? I thought it was going to be the new doll I showed you. I don't even like blue. You can keep your old crummy dress." She threw herself on the sofa and started crying.

Holly, stunned, left the room. Jim went to soothe his daughter.

"Now, don't cry. We'll get the doll this afternoon. I'm sorry I disappointed you. Don't cry." As he rubbed her back, she stopped crying.

Holly was hurt, disappointed, and angry, especially when her husband took the child's side and wasn't sympathetic to her feelings. She was especially mad when Jim bought the doll that afternoon for Kitty. All weekend, she remained quiet and distant from both her husband and his daughter.

Jim has fallen into a familiar trap where many fathers find themselves caught between wife and child. Holly probably needs to lower her high expectations, as well.

Making It Easier

There are no shortcuts to establishing a good "step" relationship. At best, it takes time and patience. Being over-eager to make a good impression is a common mistake and can lead to disappointment. Insincere interest and pushing will make matters worse, slow up progress, and only delay acceptance.

The new stepparent will probably be more successful by taking time to become acquainted with the stepchildren before trying to move in. If the stepparent has not been exposed to children of this age before, he may need to "bone up" on age levels, expectancies, abilities, and interests. It is probably wise to let the child take some of the initiative to get closer.

Some suggestions for making stepparenting easier are:

- It is best to wait at least two years after breaking one relationship before jumping into another. This gives everyone time to get unhooked from the past and recover from the depression which inevitably follows divorce or death. It also enables each person to establish emotional independence: to know his needs, strengths, and values. Children also need time to get themselves prepared. Don't spring any surprises.

- It is also better if the couple moves to neutral territory where there are no ghosts of the past—traditions, reminders, and memories—and each has an equal advantage.

- Don't marry so that your children will have another parent, but so that you will have a spouse. That is the only thing you can count on. Then make that relationship your primary force. Preserve and nurture it. Get away together. Shore up your sense of togetherness.

- Discuss ahead of time how you are going to handle problems and then talk out your differences when they arise so that you present a united front.

- Don't expect too much too soon. Keep a safe distance at first and allow the new relationships to develop slowly. Let the children decide what to call you.

- Work out the limit of your responsibilities with your spouse.

Childhood
Stress

Clearly draw the lines as to what is expected of you. Don't wait until the resentments have built up.

- Give the turf back to the stepchildren when you can. Remember it was one time theirs and you took it away. Encouraging your spouse to spend time alone with them will cut down on their need to compete.

- Don't let the children become too powerful. Don't ask permission to marry, move into a new house, change schools.

- If the stepmother works and the father is paying child support and alimony, it might be wise for her to keep out of her pay the identical amount he is paying, to be able to spend in any way she chooses.

- Don't demand the stepparent to show an emotion he doesn't feel. This will only lead to artificiality or rebellion.

- Don't overcompensate. If you feel that your spouse is not being fair to your children, don't indulge them just to get even. This will bring about increased alienation.

- Provide an atmosphere where the children are free to ask questions and to express themselves. Give them straight, honest answers without implications or elaborations. Make sure they feel important and needed.

- Don't run down the biological parent, no matter how much you are tempted. This will only broaden the distance between you. Trying to hide your jealousy will endear you to the children. Expect some comparison.

Living "in step" is not trauma all the time. It can be painful but rewarding, tricky but challenging, scary but worth it. Hang in there. It does get better.

When Laura, 10, and Karen, 9, had first been told that their parents were marrying each other, they were excited. They had been good friends for a long time. In fact, before Laura's father had died and Karen's mother had gotten divorced, the families used to vacation together.

However, after the marriage, things changed. Laura and Karen now had to share a room in what used to be Laura's house. Karen no longer got to sleep with her mother, and Laura no longer got to go places alone with her father. The girls had begun to fight over everything—who got the best grades, the most new clothes, the front seat of the car, the last piece of cake.

It was Saturday morning, and Laura's father had gone fishing.

"Come on girls, I need you to help me clean up the house," Karen's mother had said shortly after breakfast.

Laura kept watching television while her stepsister went to make her bed.

In a few minutes, Karen's mother came into the den. "Laura, I expect you to help. It's not fair for Karen to be working and you to be watching TV."

"I don't want to do chores. I never had to before. Daddy had a maid, and he never made me make my bed or clean bathrooms or vacuum. You can make Karen work, but you can't make me. You're her mother, not mine. It's no fun since you moved in with us. Before, Daddy would have taken me fishing with him, but now he makes me stay home with you and Karen. It's not fair. I used to do a lot of things with him before you two got married. Now he doesn't take me anywhere." Laura buried her head into a pillow on the sofa and started crying.

Her stepmother left the den.

Karen helped her mother with the chores and Laura kept watching TV.

When two families try to blend, many new problems surface.

It is natural for children to be jealous for they often feel displaced, neglected, or unwanted. The position they enjoyed before the marriage (the only, the oldest, smartest, cutest) is bound to be challenged.

According to Claire Berman in *Making It as A Stepparent: New Roles, New Rules* (Doubleday, 1980), seventy-five percent of all divorced and widowed women and eighty percent of men in the same situation remarry within three years. Forty-four percent of all remarriages end in divorce.

This is sad because, if the problems are handled delicately, there are reasons to believe that stepfamilies can be more successful and happy then first-time families. Because both partners are older, wiser, and more mature, they are usually more determined to make sacrifices and compromises and thus make the marriage work.

Listed below are some suggestions for couples who are considering blending two sets of children:

- Let the children in on plans as soon as possible. Don't plan to surprise them.

- Discuss arrangements and possible problems ahead of time, making sure to get input from the children.

- Create new lifestyles and rituals rather than repeating patterns of one of the former marriages.

- Plan activities which include everyone.

- Plan periodic activities for the original set: father and daughter go fishing, and mother and daughter go shopping.

- To cut down on competition and jealousy, give children tasks to accomplish together that will require cooperation: baking cookies, planning meals or trips.

- Plan regular family meetings to air grievances, discuss feelings (fear, stress, competition, jealousy, resentment), and make plans. Emphasize the need for compromises and cooperation.

- Encourage, allow, and reinforce supportive behavior from stepsiblings. Be grateful for small successes.

Try to establish a strong base and let the children know that everyone is committed to making it work. Discourage the notion that "we can throw in the towel and leave if the going gets rough." By your words and actions, teach that, in this family, problems will be dealt with and solved.

Encourage the individuality and specialness of each child. Be sure that he feels valued, develops skills, and believes in his basic goodness, importance, and individuality.

Remember that where there is desire, work and love, most things are possible.

> Sharon, 12, was coming to spend several weeks with her father and stepmother.
>
> When they met her at the airport, they hardly recognized her. She had four pierced earrings in each ear and so much makeup on her face that she looked like she was ready for the stage.
>
> "My God, Sharon, is that you?" her father stammered, as he awkwardly reached out to hug her.
>
> She giggled, "Of course, Daddy. Who did you think it was?"
>
> "Well, I thought it was some movie star getting ready to go for a screen test," said Eileen.
>
> "Don't think you are getting in the car looking like that, young lady," Carl continued, "let's get this straight right now. That makeup comes off and the extra earrings, too. Eileen, take her in the ladies' room and help her get that mess off her face."
>
> "Daddy! Don't be so old-fashioned. Mom bought this makeup for me and she says I look prettier with it on. You're not my mother," she said, turning to Eileen.
>
> "I know I'm not, and I'm glad of it," Eileen retorted, "but I agree with your father. You're not setting foot in my house looking like that."
>
> She took Sharon by the arm and led her to the ladies' room where she demanded that she wash off her face.

This summer's visit began on a negative note. Sharon was furious with her father and stepmother before they even reached home. The stage was set for a miserable visit.

No two sets of parents have exactly the same standards, and when a child has to live by different values and rules, there is a need for an adjustment period.

Understandably, Carl and Eileen were shocked to see what they considered to be the child's inappropriate appearance. However, it would have been better if they could have given themselves a little time to think through the best way to handle the situation.

Certainly Sharon was testing them, and they took the bait.

Perhaps if they could have waited until they had gotten home, settled in, and had a chance to become re-acquainted, they could have taken time to discuss rules, expectations, and standards of behavior, like:

"Sharon, what your mother allows you to do is between the two of you, but while you are living in our home, it is necessary for you to honor our rules and standards. If you want to stay with us, you will have to agree to obey our wishes.

"We want this to be a pleasant time for all of us, and we want to make compromises when possible. We do not feel that you are old enough to wear makeup, but we will allow some lipstick and mascara. Let's discuss other rules and expectations before more problems come up."

It is important for families who find themselves in difficult situations such as this to expect and allow time for testing, new adjustments, anger, jealousy, antagonism, distrust, resentment, and unpredictable mood swings.

They should not be devastated when things don't work out, remembering that all personalities are different and it takes time to understand one another. They shouldn't allow themselves to feel guilty when there are upsets. Remember, all families have their bad days.

The child needs to feel loyal to his own parent and to think well of him, whatever and wherever he is. No matter how close the child is to a stepparent, he still needs, for his own good, to think well of the separated parent. The stepparent needs to develop a new relationship with the child built on understanding, trust, and sensitivity.

George, 15, came to spend the summer with his father and stepmother. They told him that they expected him to keep the lawn mowed.

"George," his stepmother said, "it's Saturday and the grass is getting too tall. You promised to keep it cut, and it has been a long time since you touched the lawnmower."

"It doesn't need cutting. It's only been a week. If you cut it so much, it turns brown and dies. I'll cut it as soon as it needs it."

"George, I'll give you $5.00 if you'll cut it today and clean up your room. It looks like a pig sty. We are having company tonight and I want the house to look nice."

"I don't need $5.00. Grandmother gave me money before I came and she said to call her if I need any more."

"Well, don't make any long-distance calls on our bill, young man."

"Don't worry. I won't. I'll reverse the charges. She doesn't care. She isn't tight with her money. Anyway, she loves to hear from me."

Martha gave up and cut the grass herself.

A stepmother has a right to expect her stepson to pull his weight while he is staying in her home.

When he first arrives, it would be wise to have a long talk. She needs to tell him that it is important to get some things straight before the summer begins. She can tell him that he is welcome in her house, but she must insist on certain behaviors and must ask him to respect her needs and wishes.

For example, there are things she needs him to do: mow the grass once a week, keep his room clean and straight every day, trash carried out twice a week, dishes washed or dried four times a week, bathroom cleaned.

Then, she might ask him to list the privileges he would like to have. Would he like to go out with his friends every day, to the pool, to the movies, to the beach? How much would he like to be able to watch TV? What special places would he like to go? With whom? Together they might write down all the things he would like to have or be able to do.

Then they can draw up a contract, spelling out the terms carefully. In order to have the privileges he wants, he will be expected to earn them. Since money is not enticing him, it would not help to pay him for chores. (Too often when children are offered money for household chores they conclude that they have a choice—to make the money or not to make it. We don't want them to get the mistaken notion that they have a choice in the matter of chores.)

The contract may include the following:

George may not talk on the phone until the trash is carried out. He may not make plans to go out of the house until his room is cleaned. He may not go out on the weekend until the grass is mowed (no exceptions made). If it looks as if it is going to rain, he had better hurry to get the grass mowed if he wants to go anywhere. He may not watch TV until the dishes are washed.

Now comes the hard part. She will have to be tough and carry through with consequences the first time he "forgets." She will need to be very firm. "I'm sorry, but you may not talk on the phone, watch TV, go out." She does not need to threaten more punishment, yell, fuss, or lose her cool. Just remain firm.

At first, he may grumble, complain, test her and try to get by. If she is firm and consistent, he will get used to the rules and they will become second nature to him. Living together will become more pleasant for all of them.

Step-Life
Blending

This may sound simple, but it isn't. The mistake most parents (and stepparents) make is that of consistency. Some days they don't enforce the rules, other days they expect obedience. Children will do what works to their advantage.

This approach will take time at first. The stepmother will have to be alert and "catch" him if he slips up. She cannot afford to make any exceptions.

It is my feeling that, for the most part, children do not have enough required of them. Therefore they get into sloppy habits and expect others to do the work for them. This leads to resentment, hostility, handouts, and helplessness. No one profits.

Living together works better when family members are able to talk over conflicts and problems and bring them out in the open. It helps if they maintain a sense of humor and don't take themselves too seriously, realizing that many of the existing traits they find in others they cannot alter. They need to do the best job they can and accept those things they cannot change.

If the stepparent creates an atmosphere of acceptance, honesty, trust, fairness and harmony, then mutual respect and warm feeling will eventually follow.

Stepparenting

For children ages 4 to 8:

Clifton, Lucille. *Everett Anderson's Nine Month Long*. New York: Holt, Rinehart and Winston, Inc., 1978. Fiction.
> This book reassures the reader that a child can be loved as much after a parent's remarriage or the arrival of a new sibling as he or she was before.

Clifton, Lucille. *Everett Anderson's 1-2-3*. New York: Holt, Rinehart & Winston, Inc., 1977. Fiction.
> In this story a little boy explores his misgivings about getting a stepfather.

For children ages 8 to 12:

Bates, Betty. *Bugs in Your Ears*. New York: Holiday House, Inc., 1977. Fiction.

    This book demonstrates how difficult a parent's remarriage can be for children.

Ewing, Kathryn. *Things Won't Be the Same*. New York: Harcourt, Brace, Jovanovich, 1980. Fiction.

    This story realistically portrays the difficulty of making adjustments in stepfamilies.

Stenson, Janet Sinberg. *Now I Have a Stepparent and It's Kind of Confusing*. New York: Avon Books, 1979. Nonfiction.

    This book discusses the many aspects of the new family and allows children to see that others have the same feelings as they do.

Gardner, Richard. *The Boys and Girls Book About Stepfamilies*. New York: Bantam Books, 1982. Nonfiction.

Hunter, Evan. *Me and Mr. Stenner*. Philadelphia: J. B. Lippincott. 1976. Fiction.

    A realistic portrayal of an eleven-year-old girl and her relationship with her father and stepfather.

Jackson, Jacqueline. *The Taste of Spruce Gum*. Boston: Little, Brown and Co., 1966. Fiction.

    This book describes a young girl who is confused by the sudden changes in her life and is jealous about sharing her mother with another person.

For adults:

Rosenbaum, Jean and Veryl Rosenbaum. *Stepparenting*. Corte Madera, CA: Chandler & Sharp Publishers, 1977. Nonfiction.

    This book addresses many problems arising from the complex relationships generated by the presence of a stepparent in the family.

Thompson, Helen. *The Successful Stepparent*. New York: Harper and
Row, 1971. Nonfiction.

    This book gives insight and guidance to the problems of the
relationships between stepparents and stepchildren, as well as
between stepsiblings.

Blended families can mean new friends for children.

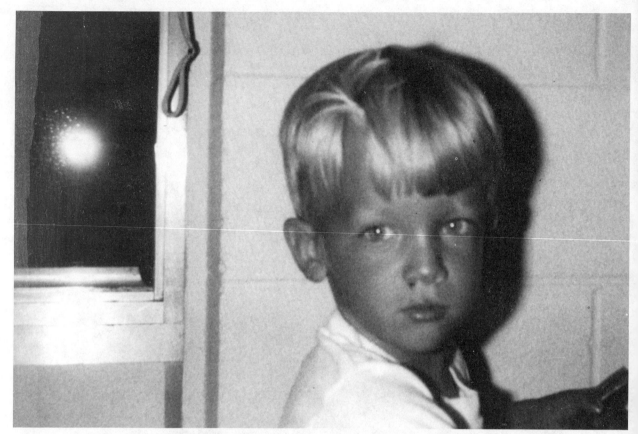

If children are going to survive this tragedy, it will be because they get help from other adults who cared enough to reach out to them.

Chapter Fourteen

Alcoholism

Only recently have the effects of family alcoholism on other family members been recognized. Until the last decade, the only help offered or available for the family was the treatment of the alcoholic himself. It was assumed that if he received help, the whole family would recover.

Now we know that is not so.

Children raised in alcoholic homes are unwilling and unwitting victims of this disease. They grow up in a home that has no order and in an atmosphere that makes no sense. Unless help is given to these innocent victims, their personalities and behavior will be affected for life.

More than half of them will either become alcoholics themselves or marry alcoholics.

These children never had a childhood. Rather, their time and energy were spent trying to control something that was uncontrollable. The whole family has joined in the conspiracy to hide the family secret by denying its very existence. These children have learned not to trust, feel or tell the truth. They often feel like they are going crazy.

To make the matter even more complicated, these children have learned masterful ways of covering up their problems and put on masks to the outside world. No one reaches out to them because no one is aware of their pain.

Fortunately, now, help is available.

Effect on the Family

Mary's father was sick again. Her brother and sister were upstairs in their rooms, but Mary, 5, was scared. She wanted to be with her mother.

Allison didn't seem to want to have Mary around and kept suggesting that she go out to play. "Can't you see that I have my hands full? Your daddy's very sick. Don't make any noise."

At the dinner table that night, Mary's dad made Mommy cry when he threw his plate on the floor and told her he couldn't eat that "garbage." Later he yelled at the children for talking, threatened to leave and never come back. . . . he even threatened to sell the children to gypsies. Finally, he passed out.

Mary fell asleep on the sofa and the next morning woke up in her bed. She tiptoed out of her room and down the stairs, where she found her mother cleaning up the floor. Her dad had gotten sick and was slumped over the table, moaning.

"Mary, you'll have to get yourself dressed for school. Get Debbie to fix your hair. I'm busy and I don't have time to help you."

Debbie came into Mary's room. "Here, I'll brush your hair. Hand me your brush."

"Debbie, what's wrong with Daddy? Is he going to die?"

"Shut up, Mary. Hurry. You'll be late for school."

Alcoholism is a *family* disease. Although usually only one family member drinks, the family balance is distorted and all other family members develop psychological or biological symptoms in an attempt to maintain the status quo.

In the United States, there are at least 28 million children, like Mary, living in homes where alcoholism daily affects their feelings, personalities, and behaviors.

In these homes, the parent's alcoholism is *the* central issue of the family. Most of the children affected have no one to help them understand what is going on, why it is going on, or how they should act or feel. Furthermore, to complicate matters even more, one of the first things they learn is to *never* talk about it. It is *the* forbidden subject. It is like a dinosaur in the living room: nobody claims to see it, yet the whole family life revolves around it. Many children raised in alcoholic homes years later attest to the fact that they never even discussed the drinking problem with their brothers and sisters.

Of course, keeping a family secret requires a great deal of skill and energy and makes it necessary for the family to isolate itself from the outside world, to put up a front at all times, and to keep other people away, to shut them out!

The biggest job of any child is to figure out what life is all about. He does this by watching, listening, testing, and evaluating his world and the people in it. His view of himself, his self-image (which he will carry with him through life), will be determined not by what actually happens to him, but rather by how he *perceives* what happens to him. In an alcoholic family, there is no way a child can make sense out of his world. Instead, all around him he witnesses unpredictable behavior. The rules the family lives by are unspoken and bizarre:

- The most important issue in the family is alcoholism.

- However, alcohol is *not* the cause of any of the family's problem.

- Someone or something else is to blame. The alcoholic can't help it.

- No one can talk about it.

- Everyone must "cover up" and "help out."

- No one ever says what he is feeling.

A child who witnesses violent rage, emotional and physical abuse, threats of murder, maniacal halluncinatory periods, vomiting, withdrawal seizures and convulsions at night, cold frosty silences, and destructive retaliations the next morning and learns that you never talk about it is forced to withdraw into a world of insecurity. Faced with an environment characterized by guilt and blame, apologies and deceit, broken promises and remorse, anger and resentment, lies and manipulations, the child develops mistrust, anger, fearfulness, and bewilderment. This fear and confusion often results in the child becoming more dependent on his parents; not trusting the unknown, he clings to what he *does* know, no matter how unsettling that may be.

To complicate matters even further, many children have to learn to deal with a parent as changeable as Jekyll and Hyde since when alcoholics are not drinking, their basic personalities are usually lovable, generous, sensitive, caring, and warm. This child is handed a dollar and given a pat on the head one day and the next day nothing he does is right. He is badgered and blamed and has his life threatened because his room is messy.

Consequently, this child becomes uncertain, unhappy, and confused. He may develop a fear of the dark or of other people. He may develop nervous disorders, eat too much, refuse to eat, learn to deceive and manipulate. He learns that honestly is *not* the best policy.

In addition, he worries silently and constantly about the health and well-being of his parents. Because of his strong dependency, he clings tighter and tighter to family members, including both the nonalcoholic and the alcoholic parent. He learns to model their crazy, nonadaptive, self-defeating coping behavior until it becomes his own.

To make it worse, the alcoholic has his anesthetic to deaden the pain when it becomes unbearable. The child has nothing and no one to help him deal with his pain.

The family had been planning all week to go to the beach on Saturday morning. Preparations were made the night before, with lunch packed and bathing suits gathered. The only obstacle was the unpredictable weather.

Jeffrey, 10, woke up early, peeked outside and found the day was beautiful—a perfect day for the beach. Hurrying to get his brother and sister up, he snuck into the kitchen to fix breakfast for everyone. Laughing, happily anticipating the day at the beach, Johnny, 9, and Julie, 6, hurried to help Jeffrey make pancakes.

Ann tiptoed into the kitchen. "Sh-sh. You're making too much noise. Bud has the flu, and I'll have to stay home to take care of him."

"But what about the beach? You promised, and so did Daddy," Johnny cried.

"I know, but I can't help it. Maybe next Saturday. Now be quiet. I don't want Bud to wake up. He'll be mad."

"That's not fair. He doesn't have the flu. I heard him come home last night. He wasn't sick then. He was screaming and throwing things. He's not sick."

"Shut up, Jeffrey. You're just like your father. You don't know when to keep your mouth shut."

Jeffrey screamed, "I am *not* like Daddy. I'll never be like him!" He ran to his room and slammed the door.

Marsha left and went to check on her husband. Johnny went out the front door, and, without saying a word, Julie picked up her doll and began rocking and singing to herself.

The Roles of Family Members

The normal and healthy development of the child requires the freedom to try different roles, to be flexible as his needs change and as he matures. The alcoholic family, however, is too insecure and fragile to permit flexibility.

Each family member feels responsible for causing the alcoholic to drink. Each family member feels responsible for coping with the problem and covering it up. Each family member feels responsible for trying to stop the drinking. These common efforts bind the family together. Like membership in a secret organization, it requires faithfulness, secret codes and messages, and strict adherance to the rules. These are the chains which bind the family together and which give it the cohesiveness and consistency which is otherwise lacking.

In order to "belong," each family member must find a niche—a role which is distinctively his to which he will rigidly adhere. Since nothing else in the alcoholic family is predictable, his role *must* remain predictable, for it becomes the key to his survival. Once adjusted to this "survival suit" the child has great difficulty managing outside of it. Most often, he carries it with him into adulthood. (Of course, this role is empty and unfulfilling because its purpose is unattainable—that of stopping the alcoholic from drinking and creating peace and harmony within the family.)

The oldest child often becomes the family hero, always striving to please. He exhibits exemplary behavior, never causes a moment's trouble. He usually grows into adulthood feeling that no matter how much he accomplishes, it is never enough. He does not feel that he has the license to feel or show anger, to relax or enjoy life. He must always strive for perfection.

Another child may become the scapegoat. He is sulky and uncooperative, seeking peer approval, negative attention and revenge. This one is the most obvious deviant, exhibiting dangerous and destructive behavior, and later becomes a potential addict or delinquent. This child is frequently labeled "born to lose" or "his father's son."

Still another child may become the "lost" child—wishing to withdraw into his own private world. She is lonely, shy, and isolated, remains emotionally detached, and frequently becomes chronically depressed and suicidal.

The youngest child sometimes becomes the mascot, seeking attention in immature ways by clowning and making other people laugh. Often this child is labeled "hyperactive" because of his short attention span.

"Rachel, where is my shirt?" her little brother called as he was getting ready for school.

"I think it's still in the laundry basket. I'll see if I can find it."

"Rachel, did you see Jon's spelling book?" Alice called.

"I was calling out his words to him last night. I think it might be on the kitchen counter."

Rachel, 12, was trying to get herself ready for school, but the questions kept coming.

"Do you know where the scissors are?" Alice called upstairs.

"They're in the drawer by the telephone."

"Is Daddy going to come with you tonight to the PTA Open House, Mama?" Rachel called to her mother.

"I hope so. I don't know. He promised to get home in time. I'm sure he will if he can get away from work."

"*You* are coming, aren't you, Mama?"

"I will if I can. You know I want to be there."

Rachel is the oldest child in a family with an alcoholic mother. Children of alcoholics never had parents who acted as parents. When these children needed help, understanding and support, or a shoulder to cry on, no one was there for them.

These children grow up to be exceptionally responsible but aloof. Since they never knew the wonder of being a child, they are relatively "joyless," never able to feel very happy or excited. Usually, they are not aware of the source of their depression. Since they are accustomed to being in control, the "responsible one," they usually marry an alcoholic—the role they know so well.

One of the sad facts about children of alcoholics is their amazing capacity

Childhood
Stress

to hide their problems. The symptoms often remain invisible because the behavior they have learned, for the most part, is approval-seeking. They go to great lengths to exhibit only socially acceptable behavior. Although they wear a veneer of being survivors, they are often miserable underneath the surface, frequently feel bad, crazy, or sick, and often suicidal.

Thirty percent of these "survivors" marry alcoholics and at least fifty percent become alcoholics themselves. If, by some stroke of luck, neither of these misfortunes strikes, many of them have alcoholic children.

Even though children may not realize a parent is an alcoholic, they know there is something wrong and that they are suffering. They can usually identify who is responsible. Sometimes, however, the alcoholic parent may be carefree and fun-loving, and the children may mistake the distraught spouse as the culprit. As the child gets older, he can see the problem more clearly.

Steps for Help

There are steps the nonalcoholic parent can take to help alleviate the pain for the children.

- Talk openly about the subject. Encourage the children to express their anger, uncertainty, fear, and guilt.

- Reassure the children that they are not responsible for their parent's problem, and they cannot cure it.

- Don't let the children suffer alone. Comfort and reassure them.

- Become educated about alcoholism. There are ways other family members "enable" the alcoholic—by covering up, protecting, and comforting. Learn how to stop these behaviors.

- Realize that only the alcoholic can decide to seek help, and that it may take a crisis to convince him. Alcoholism is a disease, not a sign of weakness, and should not be treated with disgust. Shaming the already guilt-ridden alcoholic only leads to more drinking.

- Avoid the "if you really loved us . . ." routine. It does more harm than good. Don't try to get at the alcoholic by telling him what the children or other people think.

- Don't pressure the children to take sides or push them into becoming confidants or surrogate parents. Avoid depending on the children for "adult" decisions, such as asking them whether you should leave your spouse.

- Encourage your children to become active and competent in outside activities. Arrange times when it is safe for them to invite their friends over and allow them to visit other homes so they can develop positive surrogate relationships with other adults.

- Don't make your children promise that they will never drink.

- Take advantage of community resources. There are many organizations whose purpose it is to help families of alcoholics: National Institute on Alcohol Abuse and Alcoholism; National Council on Alcholism; Al-Anon; Alateen; Alcoholics Anonymous; Women for Sobriety, Inc. P.O. Box 618, Quakertown, Pa., 18951, and National Association for Children of Alcoholics—P.O. Box 421691, San Francisco, Ca. 94142, Phone: 415-431-1366.

The family's best chance for recovery depends on the alcoholic seeking help. But even if this does not happen, the family can still learn to function in a healthy way. If the nonalcoholic parent decides to face the problem, seek help, and change the behavior patterns in the family, that parent can have a tremendous influence over the entire family. If that parent learns to strive for objectivity, compassion, and self worth, the children will be able to follow suit. Besides, seeing the other family members improve may encourage the alcoholic to get help.

Parents are not the only ones who can help their children, however. Even if the nonalcoholic parent refuses to face the problem and deal with it, there are other ways a child can get help. If children are going to survive this tragedy, it will be because they got help from other adults who cared enough to reach out to them.

The child's problem cannot be ignored. His self-concept has been formed by the way he has interpreted family events and the defense patterns that he has developed as a result of that interpretation. The work that needs to be done is to replace the existing guilt, anger, shame and unworthiness with accurate and more emotionally satisfying perceptions.

Children of alcoholics are desperate to talk about it. They need an understanding, empathic adult in whom they can trust and have complete confidence, one who can convince the child that he did not cause his parent's drinking problem.

Once the child of the alcoholic has heard and fully accepted these basic premises, he or she can be on the road to recovery.

Adult Children of Alcoholics

Sherri, 25, had been living with Jeff for two years, expecting some day to marry him. Every time she mentioned it, he said he wasn't ready, changed the subject, or got angry. She began to feel very insecure.

Lately he had been staying later at work and sometimes not getting home for dinner. He always said that he got tied up and had to work late, but when she called the office, no one answered. She wanted to believe him, but wondered if she was being taken for a fool.

When he did get home, sometimes he was out of sorts and took it out on her. One night when she asked where he had been he slapped her.

She rationalized that she wanted to trust him, so she decided not to complain and just be there for him whenever he did get home.

Sherri realized that she was gaining weight because she was eating out of frustration. She watched TV a lot or tried to fall asleep before he got home so she wouldn't constantly think about it.

Sometimes she felt she was losing her mind and at times wondered if suicide might not be a good idea. Silently, she worried night and day—there was no where to turn. Jeff was all she cared about.

Sherri was a child raised in an alcoholic family. These children were not taught to realize their own worth and know their own feelings—"Don't feel, don't trust, don't talk." They felt isolated, alienated, and different as though they deserve poor treatment and have to put up with it.

Adult children of alcoholics exhibit what is referred to as "frozen pain." They go to great lengths to avoid circumstances or confrontations which might rekindle the feelings of helplessness or rejection they felt as a child. When they become adults, they assume the same roles they developed in childhood and "play out" the same games with friends, lovers, and spouses.

Stephanie Brown and Timmen Cermak of Stanford University have developed five characteristics typical of adult children of alcoholics:

- Control: the need to control everything and everyone—not only what's happening in the outside world but what is happening within.

- Lack of trust: not only do they not trust others but they also do not trust themselves.

- Avoidance/denial of real feelings: they fear that if they are spontaneous, they will be irrational, out of control. If they love somebody, there will be heavy dependency. Intimacy is equated with being smothered.

- Sense of abandonment: Since the alcoholic is absorbed in alcohol, and the nonalcoholic is absorbed in the alcoholic, the child learns that he cannot count on anyone to take care of her or look after her needs, therefore she must put her own needs aside and look after others.

Childhood
Stress

- Overresponsibility: If anything goes wrong anywhere, it is because *she* did something wrong. Everything is her fault.

There are intervention strategies that have had remarkable therapeutic results for these children who have reported new contentment, satisfaction, and meaningful relationships in adulthood.

One of the biggest tasks for the child of the alcoholic is to learn to be his own parent—to "re-parent himself"—since he missed out on having a solid parent—child relationship. Those who have learned to do this truly find a new ability to laugh and enjoy life.

A counselor or therapist who has had experience working with families of alcoholics is usually best equipped to make connections between present pain and familial alcoholism and bring about rapid positive changes for the client.

Remarkable changes seem to come to children of alcoholics if they marry into a non—alcoholic family that is accustomed to rituals of closeness such as holiday celebrations and big family dinners. It seems that when they are able to build a new family structure in a carefully planned way, it can replace their original family, and the satisfactions are so great that the temptation to return to alcoholism is diminished.

Although there is no "cure" for the child of an alcoholic, there is, however, hope for recovery.

Alcoholism

For children ages 8 to 12:
Lee, Essie and Elaine Israel. *Alcohol and You*. New York: Julian
    Messner, 1975. Non-fiction.
        This book describes alcohol and its effects on the body. It
        also includes several chapters on relating to an alcoholic
        parent.

For children ages 12 to 16:
Schwarzrock, Shirley and C. Gilbert Wrenn. *Alcohol As A Crutch*.
        Circle Pines, Minn. American Guidance Service. Non-fiction.

The use and abuse of alcohol are raised in a series of vignettes portraying high school students

Sherburne, Zoa. *Jennifer*. New York: William Morrow & Co., 1959. Fiction.

A teenager struggles with a new school and her alcoholic mother.

Stolz, Mary Slattery. *The Edge of New Year*. New York: Harper & Row, 1974. Fiction.

This book describes the plight of a thirteen-year-old boy with an alcoholic father.

For adults:

Johnson, Vernon E. *I'll Quit Tomorrow*. New York: Harper and Row, 1973. Nonfiction.

An informative and readable book that details the symptoms of alcoholism, rationalizations and denials and intervention strategies and techniques.

The oldest child often becomes the family hero, always striving to please.

A child has complete trust in the adults who provide care and attention.

Chapter Fifteen

Crimes against Children

It should be the birthright of every child to grow up in a safe world with adults who will protect him from harm and danger until he is able to protect himself.

This, unfortunately, is not the case.

Children are not necessarily safe in their own homes, even with those who love them the most.

Because there are many mentally ill adults in our society, children are all too often innocent victims of abduction, kidnapping, abuse, and neglect. Recently, we have been startled to learn that some adults who professionally care for children are actually taking advantage of them and harming them in many ways.

Children cannot be left to learn the facts of life in their own good time. We can no longer protect them from the realities of life and allow them to remain ignorant of the possible dangers which they might encounter.

Parents need to educate their children as early as possible. They need to take every precaution to see that their children are safe and that they know what to do in dangerous situations.

Children need to be taught to respect their own bodies, to know what rights they have to privacy, and to realize that every adult is not to be trusted.

We no longer can afford to allow our children to grow up in innocence.

Kidnapping

Sarah, 4, was walking between her mother and grandmother at the shopping mall. Mother was pushing the baby in the stroller when her attention was diverted by a dress in a store window. She called to her mother, "Look, here's the kind of dress we were looking for." The grandmother turned and walked back to the window.

Very quickly, a man and a woman came up on either side of Sarah, picked her up by her elbows, and carried her into another store. They walked briskly through the store toward the exit door at the far end.

Sarah was stunned. She looked behind her to see if her mother was coming. Not seeing her, she started crying.

The lady started talking to her in quiet tones, "Be quiet, little girl, and we won't hurt you."

Fortunately, a store clerk happened to notice the strange sight. Feeling that something was amiss, she screamed, "Put her down. Help, someone!"

Frightened, the man and woman put Sarah down. They ran out the back door.

The store clerk hurried over to the child. "What is your name?" she asked.

"Sarah."

"Where is your mother?"

"I don't know."

The clerk took the child to the mall office. Soon Sarah's name was called over the loudspeaker, and in a matter of minutes her mom and Grandmother appeared. They had been beside themselves with fright, searching everywhere.

Even though this child was abducted for only a short time and was soon found, the effects of this scare lasted for a long time. It was years before Sarah would set foot in a shopping mall again. She became afraid of strangers and new places. She didn't want her mother to leave her to go to work, shopping or anywhere.

All parents live in horror that their child might be kidnapped. It can happen to any child at any time. Child Find, Inc., a nonprofit organization dedicated to finding missing children, suggests these measures to prevent abductions:

- Make sure that all children up to the age of six are kept under adult supervision at all times.

- Don't leave children in vulnerable places such as parked cars, public bathrooms, or shopping malls.

- Suggest to children that they "buddy-up" when they are away from home. A child alone is an easy victim.

- Even though children should be taught to be polite to adults, they should be reassured that they never have to say "yes" or do anything that makes them feel uncomfortable or afraid. It is perfectly acceptable to say, "No, thank you."

- It is a good idea for the family to adopt a "family code word." The children can be taught that they should never go anywhere with an adult unless the code word is used.

- It would be wise to let a child practice screaming, "Help, I'm being kidnapped," in case he found himself in a scary situation.

- Teach children how and where to report any unusual event such as a car following them or a stranger lingering beside a door or outside the school.

- Teach a child his telephone number and how to make long distance calls as soon as he is able to learn (about age four).

- Take your child to have his fingerprints recorded.

- Discuss the possibility of kidnapping with your children and let them problem-solve what they would do if . . . .

A kit called "The Child Finder" includes material on how to talk to children about kidnappings, ways to protect them from abductors, step-by-step advice on what to do if a child is missing, and an identification folder and registration card to be used in the event of abduction. For more information, write: The Child Finder, Box 277-WD, New Paltz, N.Y., 12561.

Molestation

Edward, 10, had been a member of the scout troop for two years. He and his neighborhood friends had joined the scouts when a young man in the church had volunteered to be the scout master. The parents were delighted that they would have a troup in the neighborhood with such a fine young Christian man leading it.

Richard had gone out of his way to be a good scout leader. He had taken the boys canoeing, on camping trips, and to the mountains. He met with them once a week and, in addition, volunteered to be their youth leader on Sunday nights.

One day, Edward's father called the parents of the other boys and asked them to come by his house that night. When they arrived, he told them he had bad news. Edward had confided in him that Richard was molesting the boys in the scout troop. He said that when they went on camping trips, he made them take off their clothes and he took turns playing with their genitals.

The other parents were disbelieving.

"That couldn't be so," one of them said. "I'm sure my son would have told us if Richard had been doing that. I think Edward has a dirty mind and an active imagination."

"I think you had better talk to Edward and tell him that it is serious business making accusations about another person that way. He could be sued for slander," said another parent.

Most of the other parents expressed the same sentiments.

"We had better keep this quiet. This talk could ruin Richard. He is such a fine young man. Who else could we have found that would have been so generous with his time and energy? He has spent a lot of his money on these boys too."

When the parents left, Edward's father felt quite upset. He had never known his son to lie, and he didn't believe that he would make up such a story.

The next morning, he went to the police. Fortunately, there was a detective on the force who specialized in child molesting. He took Edward's story seriously. He called the other boys in and, with some careful handling, got the truth out of them.

Edward's story had been accurate.

Any sexual activity imposed on a child under the age of twelve by an adult or adolescent is considered a sexual assault. This can be anything from an obscene phone call, exhibitionism, and fondling to oral sex and intercourse.

Pedophilia refers to people who love children in a sexual way. Pedophiles are men or women who are sexually attracted to children, either male or female.

There are two types of child molesters:

- the fixated molester whose primary sexual interest is in children. (he usually chooses boys as victims.); and
- the regressed molester whose primary sexual interest is in adults, but who turns to children, usually girls, when his adult relationships are troubled.

There is a difference between child molesters and child rapists. Child molesters are nonviolent, and they usually coax or pressure children into sexual activity. Ninety percent of sexual assault on children is committed by molesters. Child rapists use violence or threats of violence to overpower children.

Although the assaults on boys are not reported as often as those on girls, boys and girls are at equal risk. It is estimated that one out of every four girls and one out of every ten boys will be victimized sexually at some time during their childhood.

Children between the ages of eight and twelve are at the greatest risk because this group has more independence and less supervision than younger children, and, for the most part, are still fairly naive about sex.

Between eighty and ninety percent of child molesters are persons the child knows and trusts. Forty percent of assaults are committed by a parent, stepparent, or a foster parent. A child rapist is much more likely to be a stranger.

Child molesters aren't necessarily insane, retarded, drug-addicted, alcoholic, homosexual or "dirty old men." Most of them *are* men, but aside from their deviant sexual behavior, they are just like other men. They lead an otherwise respectable life and, in fact, like Richard, they are often the "do-gooder:" the one who goes out of his way to help others.

Most assaults occur during the day, often in the child's or offender's home, in a car, or elsewhere in the child's neighborhood. The molester entices, manipulates, and deceives the child into participation and usually cautions him or her not to disclose "their secret."

Sometimes the molestation continues for months or years, only to be broken off when it is discovered accidentally or when the child tells an adult who believes him. It is rare to find that a child is lying about sexual abuse, although many adults want to believe that the child made it up and will not believe his story.

Some of the signs that may indicate that a child has been molested are:

- Exhibition of sexual behavior or knowledge inappropriate for the child's age. (You would begin to wonder how they learned that).

- Exhibition of a variety of stress symptoms: fear of the dark, nightmares, stomachaches, headaches, sudden reticence to go to a certain place, or with a certain person.

- Change in the behavior of the child: an outgoing child suddenly becomes withdrawn and shy; a child who has always made good grades starts bringing home low marks; a child who has always been obedient begins misbehaving.

Since most molesters don't stop with one child, any incident (even a suspected incident) should be reported to the child protection agency and police.

Children who have been molested are plagued with guilt, fear, and low self-esteem. Many of them have sexual hang-ups which last throughout their entire lifetimes. A majority of prostitutes, drug abusers, and child molesters were molested themselves during their childhoods.

The single biggest factor which aids and abets this crime is the child's ignorance. The reason that molesters are successful in "luring" children is that children are by nature curious about sexual matters. Therefore, by neglecting to educate our children we are putting them at greater risk, playing right into the hands of the child molester.

A child who has been molested needs and deserves help and attention. Adults who care need to:

- talk to the child in private. Be patient, understanding, and sympathetic;

- assure the child that you love him, that you will continue to help and support him;

- be careful not to get angry about the situation in front of the child;

- get medical attention for the child, if necessary;

- notify the police;

- be very careful *not to blame the child in any way*. Don't chide or scold with, "Why didn't you come straight home?" "What were you doing there anyway?" "If you had only listened, this would have never happened";

- get the child professional help, if necessary;

- encourage future communication: don't just drop the subject and hope he will forget about it;

- watch for signs of distress in the future;

Parents United, Daughters & Sons United (408-280-5055) and Society's League Against Molestation (SLAM) (714-865-2151) have been organized to help families victimized by molestation.

Sexual Assault

Delores, 12, was invited to a party next door at her best friend's. "Can I go, please? she asked her parents at the dinner table.

"I don't see why not," her mother said. "What do you think, honey?"

"No. I don't think you should go because we don't know what kind of party it is, or what will be going on. You're too young to go to parties."

"Aw, Dan, it's just a children's party. Jenny's parents are going to be there. I'm sure they'll supervise. I certainly trust them," Marie said.

"No, and that's that."

Delores was upset. She went to bed early that night.

Marie went to bed too.

After she had been asleep for about an hour, Marie woke up and heard talking. She got up and went in the hall. The voices were coming from Dolores's room. She went over to the door, and started to open it. Then she stopped.

She heard Delores saying, "Don't Daddy. Stop. That hurts."

Marie froze in her tracks.

After she pulled herself together, she pushed the door open. There she saw her husband in bed with her daughter. Feeling sick to her stomach, she screamed, "Get out of here. Get out of this house!"

Dan tried to defend himself. "I wasn't hurting her. I was just rubbing her back. I knew she was mad at me for not letting her go to the party. I could hear the other children next door having a good time, and I came in to tell her I was sorry that I couldn't let her go to parties. I was trying to explain that it was for her own good. I was rubbing her back to make her feel better. Wasn't I, Delores?"

Delores didn't answer.

Seven percent of child abuse and neglect reports concern sexual abuse, (incest, molestation, rape, and exploitation). It is estimated, however, that ninety-eight percent of these incidents go unreported, and sexual abuse is the one which is *least reported*.

There are many reasons why sexually abused children keep this a secret. Often, the offender is a member of the child's household, a parent, relative, neighbor, or close friend. A younger child won't say anything because he thinks that all people behave this way. To him, there is nothing out of the ordinary about it.

Older children don't tell, because they are afraid that they might not be believed, or that it would break up their families, or that the offender might have to go to jail.

The two best ways to begin to help this problem, which has reached epidemic proportions, are to:

- increase children's awareness by providing them with information and suggestions for self protection.

- encourage children who are sexually abused to report the incidents of abuse.

Recently, governmental organizations have become aware of this alarming problem and have begun to develop programs aimed at providing instructional materials regarding sexual abuse.

One of these programs is called "Don't Touch," and was developed for children up to age nine. (Studies indicate that the majority of child sexual abuse begins around this age.)

With the use of a coloring book, children learn about "touches." There are "green flag" touches that feel good, and "red flag" touches that are bad and confusing. This program is also designed to help children know who their community support people are, how to handle potential problems and how to communicate with their parents about sexual abuse. It includes in-service training for social workers, teachers, law enforcement officers, and other groups interested in addressing this important issue.

In 1981, a play entitled *Bubbylonia Encountered,*, was produced in collaboration with the Kansas Committee for the Prevention of Child Abuse and the Johnson County Kansas Mental Health Center, targeted at children aged eight to twelve.

In 1982, ODN Productions, Inc., of New York, created a film entitled, *No More Secrets*, showing children seven years and older how to protect themselves from sexual abuse.

All of these programs are aimed at helping children to learn how to say "no," and when to say "no." They emphasize that children are in no way to blame for sexual assaults which others impose on them.

Children need to be told early in life that they have their own private areas (the ones covered by bathing suits) and that no one *ever* has the right to touch those parts of their bodies or ask them to take their clothes off.

They always need to know that they have the love and support of other adults and will not be blamed when they come to them in confidence. Only by educating the public in general, and children in particular, can we ever hope to begin to solve this giant problem of sexual abuse.

Child Abuse

Virginia was talking with her friend at the front door. Gina, 5, was in the house, supposedly watching television. All of a sudden, the women heard a scream and saw flames coming from the kitchen.

They rushed to investigate and found Gina standing by a fire in the middle of the kitchen. She had apparently gotten hold of some matches and set the dishtowels on fire.

Gina's mother threw a pan of water on the flames and then slapped Gina so hard that the child's head snapped. She shrieked at the child and ordered her to her room, following behind and slapping wherever she could hit. When they got to Gina's room, Virginia threw her on the bed and beat her with a strap. Finally, she stopped and told Gina that she could not come out of her room for a week. She also told her that she could not have her birthday (which was next month). Virginia warned Gina that if she ever played with matches again, she was going to set her on fire to see what it felt like.

Gina was terrified. Not only was the fire a frightening experience for her, but her mother's verbal and physical abuse added to her fright. Being left alone in her room by an unreasonable and angry adult gave her no way to learn from her mistake or become reconciled to her mother.

Although playing with matches is a very serious matter and one which certainly needs attention, it is not a justification for the extreme way in which the child's mother reacted.

The main issue here is the over-reaction to her daughter's childish behavior and fascination with matches. Virginia needs help with her angry feelings toward her daughter. When adults lose control of themselves and inflict harsh discipline on children which is out of proportion to the misbehavior, this is child abuse.

No one knows how prevalent child abuse is in the United States, but we do know that, every four hours, one child dies from abuse or neglect. There are approximately one million cases of child abuse reported every year and probably four times that many which go unreported.

In fact, more children die from child abuse than from home and automobile accidents and from all diseases. Fifty percent of all battered babies will die as a result of their abuse. One out of every ten school children will be abused.

Child abuse can be broken down into six forms.

- *Physical abuse:* any injury to a child other than injury sustained accidentally; that is, willful cruelty and applied trauma. This includes, like beatings which cause bruises, welts or broken bones; burns from fire, hot water, or cigarettes; lacerations or abrasions; injuries to the head and skull fractures.

- *Physical neglect:* lack of proper food, clothing, medical attention, hygiene, or parental supervision and guidance.

- *Sexual abuse* (active and passive): active engagement in sexual acts with a child, or passive knowledge of such acts.

- *Verbal abuse:* the use of insulting, coarse, or bad language about or to the child.

- *Emotional abuse:* including all of the above; the child who is emotionally abused is made to feel worthless, unappreciated, and unloved. Surprisingly, emotional abuse can be even more damaging in the long run than physical abuse.

- *Emotional neglect:* the child is shown no feelings at all, neither anger nor warmth, neither hate nor love. He is neither held closely nor spanked. It is as if he does not exist. He receives the message from his parent, "Don't bother me with your life."

This child, who is treated like a nothing grows to regard himself as a nothing—a zero.

The effects these various forms of abuse have on children are numerous. In addition to the obvious physical injuries, there are many unseen effects such as mental retardation, brain damage, physical retardation, neurological problems, psychological problems, and growth failure. Infants who are abused actually "fail to thrive" and sometimes die. Fifty percent of all physically abused children will experience significant delays in speech, language, mental abilities, motor skills, and learning ability.

Most of the time, one particular child in the family is singled out for abuse. It may be that, for some reason, he is different. He may be retarded, hyperactive, or have a birth defect. He may just remind the parent of someone he doesn't like—maybe even himself. Premature babies can be targets for abuse because there was not an opportunity for the normal parent-child bonding to occur.

If a child only receives attention when he is abused, he will sometimes actually goad the parent into abusing him by behaving in ways he knows will aggravate the abuser. Children who have to do this to get attention can grow up to be violent, to feel isolated, unloved, and inadequate.

An abused child is in double jeopardy. Not only does he have the abuse to adapt to but he also has the uncertainty of his environment—not knowing when abuse will occur. Abused children usually adapt to their environment in one of three ways:

- Hypervigilance: constantly watching adults; supersensitive to sudden noises, movements or changes in the environment; trying to protect themselves at all times.

- Constant restraint: withdrawing and trying desperately to restrict their behavior. Since abusive adults are easily provoked, it takes great effort on the part of the child to deny his natural inclination to explore, to take initiative, and to exercise his growing autonomy.

- Role reversal with parent—becoming the parent to the parent: If he is "good" (cooks, cleans, cares for the children, stays out of the way and remains quiet) he is more likely to be safe and accepted. The child's own needs are not acknowledged, his sense of self is never developed, and the normal tasks of trust, autonomy, initiative, and imagination are overlooked.

When children are rejected by their parents and their emotional needs are unmet, they learn to reject themselves.

Eight-year-old Eric, was hard to get out of bed. His mother called him several times.

His father, hearing his wife's repeated efforts, decided to take matters in his own hands. He came into Eric's room, yanked the covers off his son, and said firmly, "Son, do you want to start the day off with a beating?"

Eric immediately sprang out of bed. He didn't say a word to his father.

At breakfast his father seemed in a bad mood. He accused his mother of cooking the eggs too long. "You know how I like my eggs."

Eric, who hadn't touched his breakfast, asked to be excused from the table.

"What's wrong with you? You haven't eaten what your mother fixed for you." He reached over and slammed Eric back down into his seat. "Do you want the belt, boy?"

Eric tried to eat. He wasn't hungry. He fiddled with the food on the plate.

His father was watching. "O.K. that does it. Go to the bedroom. Get the belt."

"I'll eat," Eric protested.

"You had your chance. Go!"

Eric obediently went to the bedroom. He got the belt, handed it to his father, and leaned over for a beating?"

Abused children:

- hope that their parents will be in a good mood but are always afraid that they won't be.

- hope that they can just get through breakfast and leave for school without getting hit or hurt.

- hope that no one notices their black eyes, bruises, and stitches.

- are never sure of the consequences of a request, facial expression, or gesture. One day a request for a soft drink might be okay, while another day it might be treated as an ungrateful, selfish, greedy act and proof of an irresponsible lack of concern for the cost of living.

- worry about what is going on at home every time they are away and how things will be when they get back.

- try to think up good reasons for not bringing friends home.

- try to figure out why they deserve such treatment when brothers and sisters do worse things and get by with it.

- are careful never to laugh or cry very loud.

- feel guilty that they cause so much grief to their parent.

- hope that maybe they were adopted and that their "real" parents will some day show up to rescue them, but then . . .

- worry about what would happen to their parents if they weren't around.

Eighty percent of the people who abuse children were abused themselves in the same form when they were children. Most people learn how to parent from their own parents, and therefore, an abusing family creates a cycle of abuse that is passed down from generation to generation. Parents will react to their children instinctively as their own parents reacted to them.

The following are characteristics which are usually seen in parents who abuse their children:

- They were abused as children.

- They did not receive much love or emotional support; they had no one they could depend on.

- They don't have family, friends, or neighbors they can call on for help.

- They have a low opinion of themselves, a sense of failure or unimportance.

- They are physically ill, alcoholic, or addicted to drugs.

- They feel unwanted, unloved, unappreciated.

- They are overwhelmed with parenthood and feel they can't cope.

- They expect too much from their child—physically, mentally, or emotionally. They do not have an understanding or knowledge of child development. (When abusers are asked at what ages they expect certain behaviors, they are typically very misinformed. For example, one mother reported that she intended to start toilet training as soon as the child was born. Many others stated that they thought six months would be the appropriate time.)

- They feel that their child doesn't like them.

- They feel that their child is a "trouble maker," cries too much, is hard to manage, is "bad," and deserves to be punished.

- They feel disinterested, detached, and uncaring at times when their child is in distress.

- They continually blame or belittle one child.

- They find themselves punishing their child for minor infractions, especially when *they* are frustrated or angry.

- They believe that harsh, physical punishment is the only way to discipline.

- They realize that they sometimes lose control once they begin to punish and can't stop when they know they should.

- They feel angry or defensive when others show concern about their child, and find themselves making excuses for injuries or problems.

Child abuse occurs in all strata of society, from the very rich to the very poor. All of us are potential abusers, for all of us feel angry and highly frustrated with our children at times and have the desire to strike out against them either verbally or physically. For various reasons, it is more difficult for some to control these impulses than it is for others.

There is help available for child abusers.

The first step to a cure is to admit that there is a problem and then to seek help. There are many agencies equipped to offer immediate assistance. There are social service agencies; hotlines; counseling for parents, children and families; day-care services; emergency shelters for children (and battered wives); courses in parent education; self-help groups; support groups; and church groups.

If you are aware of abuse, you are *obligated* to report the child to someone who will investigate and lend help of a permanent nature. A report can be made anonymously.

Also, you should, if possible:

- Talk to the abuser.

- Listen, without blaming and judging.

- Offer to baby-sit and give the parent a "breather."

- Suggest possibilities for help.

- Offer to make an appointment and accompany her on the first visit.

No parent wants to be a child abuser. She needs help. If those who are informed reach out to help, a child's life may be saved.

The toll-free number which you can call twenty-four hours a day and seven days a week is 1-800-552-7096.

Additional information can be obtained by writing:

> The National Center on Child Abuse & Neglect
> P.O. Box 1182
> Washington, DC 20013

Child Abuse

For children ages 4 to 8:

Dayee, Frances S. *Private Zones*. New York: Warner Books, 1982. Non-fiction.
> A general guide which teaches children about sexual assault. It is recommended that parents read this book first.

Stowell, Jo and Mary Dietzel. *My Very Own Book About Me*. Spokane, Wash.: Rape Crisis Resource Library, Lutheran Social Services of Washington, 1981. Nonfiction.
> A colorbook/workbook for children, it uses the concepts of the body's private parts and good touch/bad touch.

For children ages 8 to 12:

Wachter, Oralee. *No More Secrets For Me*. Illustrations by Jane Aaron. Boston: Little, Brown and Co., 1983. Fiction.
> This book is a combination of four separate stories each dealing with a child who is approached sexually by an adult.

For children ages 12 to 16:

Roberts, Willo D. *Don't Hurt Laurie*! New York: Atheneum Publishers, 1978. Fiction.
> This tense story untangles the inner life of an abused child, including her reasons for not seeking help.

For adults:

Adams, Carne and Jennifer Fay. *No More Secrets*. San Luis Obispo, CA: Impact Publishers, 1981. Nonfiction.

A detailed step-by-step guide for parents to use to teach children how to prevent sexual advances.

Fay, Jennifer. *He Told Me Not To Tell*. Renton, WA: King County Rape Relief, 1979. Nonfiction.

A comprehensive collection of ideas and suggestions to help parents talk to their children about sexual assault.

O'Brien, Shirley. Child Abuse: *A Crying Shame*. Provo, Utah: Brigham Young University Press, 1980. Nonfiction.

A general presentation of child abuse and neglect.

Sanford, Linda Tschirhart. *The Silent Children: A Parent's Guide To The Prevention Of Child Sexual Abuse*. New York: Anchor Press, 1980. Nonfiction.

A detailed account of molestation and offenders with unique chapters for parents with special needs (single parents, various ethnic groups, handicapped and disabled children).

When children are rejected by their parents and their emotional needs are unmet, they learn to reject themselves.

A child below the age of two will take on the feelings of the adults who care for him. If they are sad, scared, angry, or withdrawn, he will be affected by their moods.

Chapter Sixteen

Death

When a child is faced with the death of a loved one, he needs to have a loving adult who will take the time to explain it to him. Otherwise anxieties are likely to develop that may be carried into adulthood.

As with other stresses, the young child will take on the attitudes and emotions of surrounding adults. If they try to hide their feelings, the child will assume the worst—either conclude that he caused the death or that whatever happened is *so* terrible they cannot bring themselves to discuss it with him. Children may even believe they have magical powers, and if they try hard or are good enough, they can make make the death "un-happen."

A child may think that the person who died, chose to leave him because he was so bad, and may be afraid that others will choose to leave him, too. Unnecessary fears and phobias may develop unless death is dealt with honestly.

The worst thing we can do to children when there is sadness, tragedy, and death is to exclude them from what is going on. Although it is natural to want to shield them from the pain, we need to realize that they, too, are sensitive and caring and can only benefit from our attention and honesty at a time like this.

Death of a Grandparent

In the past six months, two of Daniel's grandparents had died. His parents had been emotionally involved and preoccupied during their illnesses and then were making decisions, and taking care of property settlements.

Now, Daniel's uncle is very ill and his father's job is in jeopardy. His parents did not want to share either problem, fearful that they would burden him unnecessarily. They agreed that it would be best to wait to "break the news."

Daniel's teacher was worried about him. Last year's teacher reported that he had never had any trouble. In fact, he was a model student who made good grades and seemed happy with himself.

This year was different. The teacher was not able to reach Daniel. She found him daydreaming and more often than not, his work was incomplete.

Today was report card day and she dreaded giving them out. Daniel had never made any "C's" before, much less "D's."

When she handed them out, she watched Daniel's face turn ashen and he put his head down on his desk.

When the other children were leaving, the teacher asked Daniel to stay. He began to cry.

"What's the matter, Daniel?" she asked with concern.

"I'm scared to go home. My mom's going to kill me. I know she is. I've never gotten a 'D' before. Wait until she tells my dad."

"Do you want me to call your mother, Daniel?"

"No, that's all right."

The teacher felt awful sending Daniel home with his bad report card. She felt he was bothered by something but didn't know how to deal with it.

When families are preoccupied with stressful situations such as death or illness, children are always affected. We tend to think we can spare them from reality and therefore discuss our concerns and worries when they are not around. When they come into the room, we whisper or change the subject. Instead of sparing the child, we are, in fact causing him additional worries.

Children are wonderful detectors. They sense when all is not well with us. When we fail to tell the child what is going on, this conveys one of two messages to him: "It is so bad, they can't tell me," or "It must be my fault and they don't want me to know."

Children show their anxiety in a variety of ways: some become preoccupied and therefore cannot concentrate (such as Daniel), some become depressed and withdrawn, others show their worry in their behavior (become difficult or even "too good"). Still other signs are more obvious (lying, stealing, wetting their pants, or waking up several times a night unable to sleep).

All of this behavior indicates that the child is trying to tell us something. If he could say what was on his mind, it would probably be, "What is going on here? Why have you been sad, withdrawn, secretive? Is it my fault? Where am I in your life? How important am I? Please don't forget me."

When troubles enter our lives, it is much fairer to children to include them in the conversation—to tell them what is going on, why we are sad, and what we are worried about. Children can deal with truth and reality. It is the unknown that baffles and eats away at the child, causing him to lose his zest for living.

Blame

Randy, 6, wet his bed while he and his parents were visiting Aunt Laurie. The night before, the adults had become involved in a card game, forgetting the children, and Randy had fallen asleep on the sofa. After his parents had finished their card game, they had carried their son upstairs.

The next morning, when he discovered he had wet the bed, he came into his parents' room and told them about it.

Don hit the ceiling. He was beside himself with rage. A troubled man who had recently lost his job, he shamed Randy saying, "I can't believe that you would do such a thing. How old are you, anyway? I thought you were six. I must be wrong. You must be two. Let's go out and buy some diapers today. I wonder if they make diapers big enough to fit you? Do you think so, Randy? You'll feel funny trying them on in the store, won't you?"

Randy's mother felt sorry for him. He was so ashamed and embarrassed. He said nothing.

The family left for home that morning. Off and on all day, Don brought up the bed–wetting incident to his son.

That night after Randy had gone to bed, his father committed suicide.

It was not until years later that Randy confessed his feelings of guilt over his father's suicide. By that time, no one could convince him that the reason his father had killed himself was not because *he* had wet the bed. The child had truly believed that because his dad had been so upset with him over the incident and had said so many awful things, that his fury and rage had made him want to end his life.

It took years of therapy for Randy to get a handle on his needless guilt over his father's death.

Children Randy's age think that the world revolves around them, and that they have the power to make things happen. Parents need to realize their children's vulnerability and the need to help them through these troubling times.

Marcos, 8, and his uncle were very close. Even though he had two older brothers, Marcos always felt he was "special" to his Dad's brother.

There had been no warning that his uncle was ill. He had a heart attack and died in his sleep.

That night, Marcos woke up to his mother's crying and voices in the hall. He lay very still, trying to figure out what was wrong. "Does Marcos know?" someone asked. He couldn't hear the answer.

He tiptoed to the door. His mother saw him there, drew him to her side, and told him his uncle had died during the night.

Marcos' whole world went black.

Later that day, people came to the house, bringing food. The more food Marcos saw, the sicker he felt. How could anyone eat?

Marcos wouldn't eat for days and his parents were so grief-stricken, they couldn't deal with him. Finally, they decided to send him to spend several months with his cousins.

It was the beginning of years of sadness for Marcos. He lost a lot of weight that summer and became sullen and withdrawn. When he started back to school, he had trouble with all his subjects. His handwriting became illegible, and he couldn't concentrate. The teachers didn't know what to do. He failed the third grade.

It is not unusual for life to be temporarily shattered when there's a death in the family, especially when it is unexpected.

Adults sometimes make an attempt to protect children from grief by not talking about the subject in front of them or sending them away until things are "back to normal."

Children, however, should *not* be protected from grief. It is even more devastating to them to be excluded from the trauma—they have feelings that need to be expressed. Just because a child doesn't ask questions or show distress on the surface doesn't mean he is unaffected or is "taking it well."

A child needs to stay in familiar surroundings where he can depend on those who love him. He should be allowed to see them mourn because he will learn from their reactions. He should be encouraged to talk, ask questions, and be sad. These are the normal processes which will help him work through the shock and resume a normal life.

Adults should never assume the child is too young to understand. He needs to learn that sadness and death are part of life. His coping skills will be learned from observing those of adults around him.

Children should be allowed to take part in funeral arrangements. It is also a good idea to let them decide if and when they should visit someone who is dying. They may want the chance to say "good-bye." This can be very touching and therapeutic for all involved. Children can handle the situation much better than we would ever dream.

They will grieve, as we do, but their grief comes in small portions. Often, they will abruptly be ready to go play with friends. Young children have short attention spans and can only take in so much information before they lose interest and move on to something else. The important thing is to tell them the truth and always answer their questions honestly. As long as you are nearby to answer those questions when they arise, they'll feel safe and slowly return to normal lives while going through the grieving process.

It is best to answer children's questions in terms they can understand. Children also respond when they are given opportunities to talk about the person they loved. In the moving film, "Where is Dead?" the young child feels comforted when she tells friends and relatives that her deceased brother, David, is now a "memory," and she draws pictures and describes the things they did together.

Young children become fascinated with death and need their curiosity satisfied. They often ask questions about death. "What is death?"; "Why do people die?"; "When will you die?" "When will I die?";

"Where do you go when you die?"; "Does it hurt to die?"; "When you die, who will take care of me?"

Children take us literally. If we tell them the deceased has gone to sleep or on a trip they may be afraid to go to bed or to let others out of their sight.

It is all right to answer some questions with, "We aren't sure about some things. This is what we believe but all people don't think alike."

At all levels, children should be encouraged to work through the natural processes of grief. A prior understanding of the life cycle of plants and experiences with the death of pets would be beneficial, for they help to prepare the child for dealing later with the loss of someone who is important to him.

Death of a Parent

While she was nursing her baby in the hospital, Leanne discovered a lump on her breast. She mentioned it to her obstetrician and he examined her. He then ordered a biopsy.

The next day, he came in with the bad news that she would have to have a mastectomy and the sooner the better.

Leanne and her husband were shaken to realize that the baby could go home, but Mother would have to stay in the hospital for major surgery.

She came through the surgery fine, but the doctor warned her that she had better not get pregnant again.

Three years later, with her cancer in remission, she decided to have another child.

She was pregnant within months and, as soon as her pregnancy got under way, her cancer returned. Although she was very weak through the pregnancy, she delivered a healthy, normal child. Fourteen months after his birth, Leanne died.

This father not only had his own grieving to do, he also had to help his children deal with theirs.

A child below the age of two will take on the feelings of the adults who care for him. If they are sad, scared, angry, or withdrawn, he will be affected by their moods. He may react in different ways - by excessive crying, clinging, apathy, or irritability.

A child between the ages of three and five will not understand death as a final process, but rather as a temporary absence and may develop stronger separation anxiety for fear that others aren't coming back when they leave. Young children believe that death is only temporary, like falling asleep or taking a trip.

Children begin to comprehend that death is permanent about the age of seven. They still think in terms of death happening to "other" people but not possibly to them. They personify death as if it is represented by the boogey man, or a monster. They are afraid of the dark and think they can run and hide from death if it comes.

Not until the age of 10 to 12 does a child begin to take on an adult understanding of death, realizing that it is inevitable and will someday happen to him.

Once children begin to realize that death is actually permanent and something they cannot reverse, the anger and depression usually set in. They become angry with the person who died, or the person who allowed it to happen. They might try to take it out on God. More often than not, their anger shows up in behavior: tantrums, aggression, fighting, arguing, obstinacy.

Anger is followed by depression. To the astute observer, the child may develop pervasive sadness or apathy. Unfortunately, parents who are still caught up in their own grief, sometimes mistake the "quiet" behavior for "improved" behavior.

These children need adults who are sensitive to what they are going through. They need to be able to talk, feel, be angry, cry and express themselves. Otherwise, they will learn more ways to "act out" their frustrations (school problems, phobias, nightmares, tics, stuttering).

Given enough time, and loving support, acceptance will eventually come. When children have a loving adult who understands their needs, accepts their feelings, answers their questions, allows their outbursts but sets limits on the "acting out behavior," they almost invariably come to accept the death and take the necessary steps to get on with their lives.

Children who are forced to face grief early in their lives are often the stronger because of it. As they gradually learn to express their feelings, say "good-bye," and go on with their lives, they are gaining a more realistic view of the world and developing coping skills to deal with it.

Katherine Patterson, the celebrated children's author, tells in her book *Gates of Excellence* about the death of her son's best friend, when both children were in the second grade. Carefully she watched him move painfully through each difficult stage of grief, including the one where he determined that God hated him and would probably kill his sister next.

Finally he arrived at the final stage of acceptance, but, she says, it did not embrace full healing. She said, "Of course his life will go on, but he will never 'get over' Lisa, as you 'get over' a disease." She wrote, "I want the joy of knowing Lisa and the sorrow of losing her to be a part of him and to shape him into growing levels of caring and understanding, perhaps as an artist, but certainly as a person."

Death of a Sibling

Diana's parents had been worried about their twelve-year-old daughter for quite a while. She had always been the athletic one while her sister, Janine, 13, had settled for more passive activities.

Lately, Diana had become lethargic and seemed to be lacking energy all the time. She used to enjoy riding her bike, and taking ballet but now she rarely chose to go outside and instead flopped on the sofa and watched TV as soon as she got home from school.

Sometimes she fell asleep before finishing her homework.

Childhood
Stress

255

Her parents thought at first that she was unhappy at school. They talked to her teacher, who said that sometimes she didn't seem to have enough energy to play at recess or after lunch. She said that she had worried about Diana for some time, wondering if she might be ill.

Her parents decided to take her to the doctor. He couldn't find anything wrong, so he sent her for extensive testing.

The report came back that Diana had leukemia. The doctor told them that they should prepare for Diana to die. They were unbelieving and numb for a few days. Then they knew that they would have to break the news to Diana as well as decide what they would tell her sister.

Our society tries to shield children from the reality of death. We convey the unconscious message that death is for the very old. However, chronic illness (cancer, cystic fibrosis, leukemia, and muscular dystrophy) still causes death in children, and families need help in coping.

A child who is dying will be confused if the adults spoil her in an effort to distract her. It is very difficult to fool a child. She can sense phoniness and, if she is not told what is going on, she will assume that she has done something so bad that no one wants to talk with her about it.

These children will go through the same stages as others when they are facing death: denial and isolation, anger and rage, bargaining, depression, and acceptance. Children do not necessarily go through the stages in the same order, nor do they always continue to move ahead. Sometimes they temporarily regress to a former stage. When they are kept in the dark about their illness and impending death, however, they rarely grow beyond the first stage of denial and isolation.

The dying child needs and deserves:

- to know that he or she is dying
- an opportunity for meaningful communication
- to live to the end with dignity

- to be listened to without anger and with acceptance
- to hope
- to know that he or she is a valuable person
- not to be forgotten
- to maintain self-esteem

Up to age three, the child does not understand the permanency of death but does know what separation and loss are.

From ages three to five, the child still does not understand the permanency of death but has probably had some experience with death—a pet, a relative or a TV character. A child of this age who is terminally ill will fear death and be afraid of separation and pain. He may experience extreme guilt feelings because he thinks he must have done something awful to deserve such a dreadful thing.

The child between the ages of six and twelve understands that death is inevitable and universal. This child needs and deserves to be given the facts. If he is lied to, he will usually sense this and attempt on his own to research the facts concerning his illness.

A school-age child with a terminal illness needs to continue schooling as long as it is at all possible—needs to engage in *purposeful activity*. This will help that child maintain a good self-image and know that parents and teachers have not given up on him and still have faith in his future.

This child needs adults who will let him talk and answer questions. Sometimes he may feel that his parents are unapproachable, for they get too upset.

Parents need to keep in close touch with the school, for the teacher needs to know exactly what the child is capable of, what he has already been told, and what they want the child to know. Teachers can use the marvelous medium of a diary to help the child express his real feelings. They can also provide art and music experience through which the child can express himself. Role playing, magic circles, and play therapy are also useful.

Childhood
Stress

257

These children should be encouraged to set short-term as well as long-term goals, so that they can continue to achieve success and mastery. They may want to start giving away prized possessions to special persons in their lives, and they should be allowed to do so.

Elizabeth Kubler-Ross states that, "If a problem is faced, whether or not it can be solved, the result is growth."

Helping a child face his own mortality helps all of those around to deal more effectively with their own issues of life and death.

When there is the death of a child, usually one or both parents become totally absorbed in their own grief. This can result in additional crises in the family as one or both partners may turn to alcohol or drug abuse, illness, separation, or divorce.

Meanwhile, the needs of the remaining child often are overlooked.

This child must also handle the death, but he, unfortunately, must often do it without the parents' help. Frequently, the parents are too tied up with their own loss to be aware of the sibling's reactions, therefore forcing the child to deal with the temporary "loss" of parents as well as the loss of a sibling.

During their grief, the child may become frightened as he sees a side of his parents that he has never seen before. He may view their reactions as excessive and wonder if his death would be mourned as deeply.

Parents need to be careful not to idealize the lost child, as this is likely to damage the remaining child's self-esteem and cause him to try to imitate or replace the child who has died.

If the child who died was an adolescent, the family may have increased guilt. Adolescence is a stressful time at best, and the child may not have been on such good terms with other family members before he got sick. There could be many regrets, guilt, and blame.

It is important to remember the age of the sibling and his own limited background. His perceptions will be based on what he knows and has experienced. J.H. Arnold, in *A Child Dies - A Portrait of Family Grief*, gives examples of typical misperceptions of children who are uninformed and trying to make sense out of the death of a sibling.

Children will need to grieve for their lost sibling, for themselves, and for the changed family system. This takes time and patience. Adults need to be open, honest, and available. The remaining child needs an invitation to grieve openly.

Helpful ways other people can reach out to families who are grieving are:

- Express sympathy. Don't avoid talking about the death. That is what is uppermost in the mind of the family. Don't think it helps to distract their attention.

- Don't avoid using the name of the person who has died.

- Accept their expressions of grief.

- Encourage the family members to talk.

- Give extra attention to the children. Remember, they are hurting too.

- Be there. Show up. Don't fool yourself into thinking you won't be missed or that you might be in the way.

- Accept them where they are. Avoid trite statements like, "You need to be getting on with your life and putting this behind you."

- Don't remind them of their blessings (children, parents, friends, etc.). No one can take the place of the loved one who is gone.

- Don't try to make suggestions and decisions which are none of your business ("Why don't you get a job, have another child, get a pet, move to another house?").

- Avoid sowing seeds of doubt ("If only you had gotten her to the hospital/hadn't gone to the beach/had been home"). The bereaved are going through enough pain and self-doubt without adding more to it.

Childhood
Stress

Death

For children ages 4 to 8:

Brown, Margaret Wise. *The Dead Bird*. Reading, Mass.: Addison-Wesley Publishing Co., 1965. Fiction.

    This is a story about a dead bird that is found and buried. There is excellent sensitivity to children's feelings about death in illustration and text.

DePaola, Thomas A. *Nana Upstairs*. New York: G.P. Putnam's Sons., 1973. Fiction.

    This simple, touching story shows a close, loving relationship between a child and his great-grandmother.

Stein, Sara Bonnett. *About Dying: An Open Family Book For Parents And Children*. New York: Walker and Co., 1974. Nonfiction.

    A realistic view of death is presented through a child's experiences with the death of his pet and his grandfather.

For children ages 8 to 12:

Paterson, Katherine W. *Bridge To Terabithia*. New York: Thomas Crowell Co., 1977. Fiction.

    A friendship flourishes between a country boy and a girl from the city as each opens new experiences to the other. The girl's death inspires the boy to assert himself.

Smith, Doris Buchanan. *A Taste Of Blackberries*. New York: Thomas Y. Crowell, 1973. Fiction, 1973. Fiction.

    This book is an account of the emotions, memories, and actions of an eleven-year-old boy whose best friend dies.

White, Elyn Brooks. *Charlotte's Web*. New York: Harper and Row Publishers, 1952. Fiction.

    This book describes sorrow after the death of a close friend and shows how memories of a dead friend can keep the friend alive in one's mind.

For children ages 12 to 16:

Gunther, John. *Death Be Not Proud: A Memoir*. New York: Harper and Row Publisher, 1949. Nonfiction.

    The anguish of a father faced with the inevitable death of his son is sensitively portrayed.

LeShan, Eda J. *Learning To Say Good-By: When A Parent Dies*. New York: Macmillan Publishing Co., 1976. Nonfiction.

    This book assists young people to see clearly the range of responses they may feel to a parent's death.

Peck, Robert Newton. *A Day No Pigs Would Die*. New York: Dell Publishing Co., 1974. Fiction.

    This narrative portrays the strength of a father's influence on a boy, and the boy's deep struggle to accept death's inevitability and consequences.

For adults:

Easson, William M. *The Dying Child*. Springfield, Illinois: Charles C. Thomas Publishers, 1970. Nonfiction.

    The book highlights the tasks of facing the dying child and those who deal with him.

Griffin, Mary and Carol Felsenthal. *A Cry For Help*. New York: Doubleday and Co., Inc., 1983. Nonfiction.

    An exhaustive compilation of facts and personal histories of teenage suicides.

Rudolph, Marguerita. *Should The Children Know?* New York: Schocken Books, 1978. Nonfiction.

    This book explores death and its implications for children.

Schiff, Harriet Sarnoff. *The Bereaved Parent*. New York: Penguin Books, 1978. Nonfiction.

    The author examines real life experiences of bereaved parents and siblings and how they came to grips with their anger, guilt, and grief.

Epilogue

There is a tendency on the part of most of us to focus gloomily on the ills of society and to worry about what does and can go wrong. The key to prevention, however, lies in the more important consideration of how and why some children are *not* damaged by adversity but rather, seem to emerge from difficult times stronger and more confident than many who had less stressful childhoods.

Even in the most terrible homes, where strife and problems abound, some children appear to develop healthy, stable personalities and to demonstrate remarkable degrees of resilience.

Some researchers have become intent on discovering "What has gone *right* with these children?" and "How can we help other children to become less vulnerable when faced with life's adversities?

These researchers have studied resilient children of psychotic parents, children of divorce, uprooted children of wars, and child survivors of the Holocaust. Despite prolonged and severe psychological stresses, all of these children demonstrated phenomenal psychological strength. They appear to possess high self-esteem and strong values, sensitivity to others, successful peer relationships and school experiences, and exciting plans for their futures.

These children who have suffered early misfortunes and life stresses yet have exhibited remarkable strength and emerged with stable, healthy personalities seem to have the following characteristics in common:

- They know how to play vigorously.
- They are excited about life - they seek out new experiences.
- They are independent and self-reliant.
- They know where and how to ask for help.
- They have social skills and they are able to attract other people to them.
- They have a sense of humor.
- They have been required to look out for and help others.
- They have a close bond of mutual trust with at least one adult.
- They have developed skills, talents, hobbies, and interests.
- They have a belief in themselves and their ability to make things happen.
- They have a sense of belonging, a reason for being, a purpose for living.

When we give our children roots as well as wings, they will be like the healthy plant: when it meets an obstacle, it re-routes itself. Our children, when they have strong roots, will likewise be able to re-route themselves when obstacles appear in their path. Instead of allowing a closed door to become a stumbling block, they will turn it into a stepping stone—an opportunity for advantage, learning, strength, and growth.

Bibliography for Adults

Anthony, E.J. "The Syndrome of the Psychologically Invulnerable Child." In *The Child in His Family 3: Children at Psychiatric Risk*, ed. E. J. Anthony and C. Koupernik. New York: Wiley, 1974.

Block, Jr. "Growing Up Vulnerable and Growing Up Resistant: Preschool Personality, Pre-Adolescent Personality and

Intervening Family Stresses." *In Adolescence and Stress* ed. C. D. Moore. Washington, D.C.: U.S. Government Printing Office, 1981.

Garmezy, N. "Children Under Stress": Perspectives on Antecedents and Correlates of Vulnerability and Resistance to Psychopathology." In *Further Explorations in Personality*, ed. A. I. Rabin, J. Aronoff, A.M. Barclay, and R. A. Zucker. New York: Wiley, 1981.

Garmezy, N. "Stressors of Childhood." In *Stress, Coping and Development*, ed. N. Garmezy and M. Rutter, New York: McGraw-Hill, 1983.

Garmezy, N. "Stress Resistant Children: The Search for Protective Factors." In *Aspects of Current Child Psychiatry Research*, ed. J. E. Stevenson. *Journal of Child Psychology and Psychiatry*, Book Supplement 4, Oxford, England: Pergamon, in press.

Honig, A. "Research in Review: Risk Factors in Infants and Young Children." *Young Children 38*, no. 4 (May 1984): 60–73.

Moskovitz, S. *Love Despite Hate: Child Survivors of the Holocaust and Their Adult Lives*. New York: Schocken Books, 1983.

Murphy, L. and Moriarty, A. *Vulnerability, Coping and Growth from Infancy to Adolescence*. New Haven: Yale University Press, 1976.

Wallerstein, J. S. and Kelly, J. B. *Surviving the Breakup: How Children and Parents Cope with Divorce*. New York: Basic Books, 1980.

Werner, E. E. and Smith, R. S. *Vulnerable, but Invincible: A Longitudinal Study of Resilient Children and Youth*. New York: McGraw-Hill, 1982.

Index

I

Illness, 111
    children's misconceptions about,
        114–115
    child's, 112–116
    parental, 116
Independence, 89, 95
    training, 160–161

J

Jealousy
    sibling, 44, 49
Junk food, 32

K

Kidnapping, 228–230

L

Latchkey children, 151
    and responsibilities, 154
    possible solutions, 162
    safety tips, 156–158
Learning disabilities, 70
    suggestions for parents, 71–72
    traits, 70–71
"Learning match", 55–56, 63
Leaving home, 96
Loss, 103

M

Mainstreaming, 135
Military deployments, 79

adjustments to, 83
    re-entry suggestions, 84
Molestation, 230–234
Moodiness, 104
Moving
    easing transition, 76–77
    preparation for, 78
Modeling, 17
Motivation, 37

N

New baby, 42
    coping skills, 45

O

Overfeeding, 33
Over protection, 59

P

Parental attitude
    and physically handicapped, 126
    and teenagers, 94
    eating habits, 31
    moving, 78
    perfectionist, 67
Parents' role
    in handling stress, 13–14, 17
Power struggles, 23
Privileges
    as incentives, 52
Problem solving, 158

R

Regression, 13–14, 22, 45, 111
Reinforcing, 24
    appropriate behavior, 51
    uniqueness, 50
Rejection, 129
Resistance
    to toilet training, 19
Responsibility, 36, 61, 69, 154
Resilient children, 262–263
Rewards, 61, 69

S

Salk, Dr. Lee, 44
School problems
    changing school, 63
    need to support teacher, 59
    school phobia, 64, 92–94, 105
    separation anxiety, 57, 91–92
School success
    how parents can help, 69
Self-esteem
    bed-wetting, 27
Self-image, 215
Separation
    anxiety, 57, 64, 90–91
    coping with frequent, 81–82, 85–86
    new baby, 42
    preparing for, 43
Sexual Abuse, 230–236
Siblings, 41
    benefits of, 50
    family constellation, 47–48

of the handicapped, 133–135
    rivalry, 46, 49
    to minimize sibling rivalry, 50
Single parent, 179–193
Step-life, 195–211
    visitations, 205–209
Stress
    coping skills, 16–17
    related to academic performance, 62
    signs of, 15–16
Survival skills, 89
    for physically handicapped, 125
Suicide, 104
    teenage, 108
    tendencies, 107–108

T

Teenagers, 36, 92–96
    and adoption, 143–148
    and suicide, 108
Toilet training
    bed-wetting, 24–27
    chronic constipation, 28–29
    readiness, 20
    resistance to, 19–21
    regression, 22–24
Trauma, 141

W

Weight problems, 34
Withdrawal, 129